Welding Technology for the Aerospace Industry

Proceedings of a Conference
October 7-8, 1980
Las Vegas, Nevada

Sponsored by
American Welding Society Education Department

Welding Technology Series
American Welding Society
2501 N.W. 7th Street, Miami, FL 33125

Library of Congress Number: 80-70762
International Standard Book Number: 0-87171-214-8

Printed in the United States of America

Contents

Welding Technology for the Aerospace Industry
Conference Program Advisory Board

Gail E. Eichelman
Chief, Structural Metals Branch
Air Force Materials Laboratory
Wright Patterson AFB, OH

Mel Schwartz
Chief, Manufacturing Technology
Sikorsky Aircraft Company
Stratford, CT

Harry J. Heckler
Manager, Fabrication Technology Lab
General Electric Company
Cincinnati, OH

Yolanda Smith
Manager, Conferences and Seminars
American Welding Society
Miami, FL

Wallace J. Lewis
Design Specialist
McDonnell Douglas Corporation
St. Louis, MO

Frank J. Wallace
Chief Welding Engineer
Pratt-Whitney Aircraft Group
E. Hartford, CT

Debrah Weir
Director, Education
American Welding Society
Miami, FL

v

Preface

There are five major steps to the organizing of an AWS conference: analysis, design, development, delivery, and evaluation. AWS experts are involved in all stages of conference production but especially in the analysis, design, and evaluation phases.

The process begins with the AWS Conference and Seminar Committee, chaired by Philip D. Flenner, Senior Welding Engineer, Consumers Power Co., Jackson, Michigan. Here the concept is evolved into a proposed scope with major objectives laid out.

Next a program advisory board, representing the foremost leaders in the field, is assembled by staff. In the case of "Welding Technology For the Aerospace Industry," AWS is especially endebted to Gail E. Eichelman, Chief, Structural Metals Branch, Air Force Materials Laboratory, Wright Patterson AFB, Ohio; Harry J. Heckler, Manager, Fabrication Technology Lab, General Electric Co., Cincinnati, Ohio; Wallace J. Lewis, Design Specialist, McDonnell Douglas Corp., St. Louis, Missouri; Mel Schwartz, Chief, Manufacturing Technology, Sikorsky Aircraft Co., Stratford, Connecticut; and Frank J. Wallace, Chief Welding Engineer, Pratt-Whitney Aircraft Group, East Hartford, Connecticut, who served in this capacity so well.

At the initial program development meeting held November 1979 in Houston, the Conference Program Advisory Board refined the proposed conference scope: the conference would restrict itself to the welding processes most important to future commercial and military aeronautic framework design and construction, aircraft hardware reclamation, and materials evaluation. Processes to be covered included diffusion welding, laser welding, electron beam welding, superplastic forming, keyhole plasma arc welding, inertia welding, and resistance welding. Other topics would include weldability of critical materials and alternatives, welding supports such as adaptive controls, microprocessors, digital arc welding programmers, and the application of fracture control.

Finally, a session on repair welding was planned to round out the two-day event for a targeted audience of welding engineers, designers, metallurgists, materials engineers, and decision-making technical managers working with welding on a practical basis on the manufacturing front line.

More than 150 professionals attended the October 7-8, 1980, conference held in Las Vegas. The massive staging job was directed by Yolanda Smith, AWS Manager of Conferences and Seminars. AWS Executive Director George Weinfurtner opened the conference and talked about the long-term objectives of the AWS Conference Series, which started in February 1978.

Projections on the successful AWS series see over 7,000 engineers, technicians, scientists, quality assurance and quality control managers and personnel, production and operations specialists, and others involved in welding on a practical level attending an AWS conference or seminar by December 1981.

Several key objectives were planned for conference attendees:

- Effective sequencing of repair and rework activities
- How to increase electron beam welder capabilities using standard equipment
- Why welding improves material use
- What new process repairs engine parts with properties comparable to original materials
- How to reduce defects and distortions when butt joint welding (aluminum)
- Best way to apply fracture data when defining defect limits
- Engineering, metallurgical, and manufacturing advantages of inertia welding
- Critical differences between diffusion welding processes
- What factors must be controlled in *in situ* repair welding
- Latest applications for superplastic forming/diffusion bonding
- Role of hardfacing, welding monocrystal and equiaxed super alloys in repair
- Weld variables, equipment, and techniques for keyhole plasma arc welding
- How to tailor a weld specification to specific end use
- Newest applications for laser welding
- Latest advances in resistance welding

According to those who attended, these Advisory Board planned objectives were dead-center: 100 percent of the attendees reporting said the program was worth their time and money, and 96 percent said the content of the program was excellent to good and high in practical value.

AWS wishes to express its profound appreciation to all the speakers who volunteered their time and efforts to make this program the success it was: Jeffrey P. Carstens, Manager, Industrial Laser Dept., United Technologies Research Center; Frank S. Pogorzelski, Section Manager and Manufacturing Research Engineer, McDonnell Aircraft Co.; John R. Williamson, Deputy Program Manager, Air Force Flight Dynamics Laboratory, Wright Patterson AFB; I.B. Robinson, Head, Joining Section, Applications Research, Kaiser Aluminum and Chemical; William R. Gain, Supervisor, Manufacturing

Technology, Boeing Aerospace Co.; Dr. Robert W. Messler, Jr., Group Head, Advanced Metallic Structures Development, Grumman Aerospace Corp.; Al S. Wadleigh, President, Interface Welding; Robert Szabo, Senior Welding Engineer, Pertron Controls Corp.; Gasparas Kazlauskas, President, Astro-Arc Co.; Gregory J. Mueller, Chief Electrical Engineer, Merrick Engineering, Inc.; D.A. Bolstad, Section Chief, Materials Engineering and Fracture Control, Martin Marietta Aerospace; Thomas J. Bosworth, Senior Specialist, Boeing Aerospace Co.; Fred R. Miller, Project Manager, AF Materials Laboratory, Manufacturing Technology Div., Metals Branch, Wright Patterson AFB; John M. Gerken, Staff Engineer, TRW, Inc. (and a member of the AWS Board of Directors); Donald L. Keller, Senior Repair Engineer, Aircraft Engine Group, General Electric Co.; and Mel Schwartz, Sikorsky Aircraft.

Finally, AWS thanks Mr. Al Johnston, District 21 Director, who represented the local AWS Las Vegas Section and was instrumental in the especially rewarding recruitment of new AWS members from the conference attendees.

Debrah Weir
Director of Education
American Welding Society

Diffusion Welding

Mel Schwartz
Sikorsky Aircraft

Diffusion welding (DFW) to date has found most of its applications in the atomic energy and aerospace industries. To meet the stringent requirements of these industries, it was not only necessary to develop new materials but, equally as important, it was also necessary to develop methods to fabricate them into useful engineering components. Diffusion welding is one such fabrication technique developed to keep pace with the requirements of the advancing technology. DFW is a process that carries many names because it can be applied in a large variety of ways. The essential details of the procedures and the metallurgical aspects are the same for all forms of the process.

DFW *per se* is not a completely new joining technique. Forge welding processes have been used to join both wrought iron and low carbon steels for many years. In fact, forge welding is one of the oldest known joining methods and was the only process in common use before the nineteenth century. It is interesting to note that the famous "Damascus blade" of medieval times was made by forge welding, and the technique has even been traced back in one form to at least 1500 B.C. in the Euphrates Valley.

DFW is a solid-state process that produces coalescence of the faying surfaces by the application of pressure at elevated temperature. The process does not involve macroscopic deformation, melting, or relative motion of the parts. A solid filler metal (diffusion aid) may or may not be used between the faying surfaces. Terms sometimes used synonymously with DFW include diffusion bonding, solid-state bonding, pressure bonding, isostatic bonding, and hot press bonding.

Several kinds of metal combinations can be joined by DFW:

(1) Similar metals may be joined directly to form a solid-state weld. In this situation, required pressures, temperatures, and times are dependent only upon the characteristics of the metals to be joined and their surface preparation.

(2) Similar metals can be joined with a thin layer of a different metal between them. In this case, the layer may promote more rapid diffusion or permit increased microdeformation at the joint to provide more complete contact between the surfaces. This interface metal may be diffused into the base metal by suitable heat treatment until it no longer remains a separate layer.

1

(3) Two dissimilar metals may be joined directly where diffusion controlled phenomena occur to form a bond. The mechanisms are similar to category (1) above, with the added effects that dissimilar metals create.

(4) Dissimilar metals may be joined with a third metal between the faying surfaces to enhance weld formation either by accelerating diffusion or permitting more complete initial contact in a manner similar to category (2) above.

Another similar process sometimes confused with DFW is diffusion brazing. Diffusion brazing (DFB) is a process that produces coalescence of metals by heating them to a suitable temperature and by using a brazing filler metal or *in situ* liquid phase. The filler metal may be preplaced or formed between the faying surfaces or distributed by capillary action in the joint. Pressure may or may not be applied. The filler metal is diffused with the base metal to the extent that the joint properties approach those of the base metal. A distinct layer of brazing filler metal does not exist in the joint after the DFB cycle is completed. This characteristic distinguishes the process from brazing. The process is sometimes called liquid phase diffusion bonding, eutectic bonding, or activated diffusion bonding.

The distinction between DFW and DFB may not be clear since a filler metal may be used with both processes; however, it is understood that melting actually takes place at the faying surfaces during the early stage of a DFB cycle. The filler metal layer itself may melt or a eutectic liquid may form from alloying between the filler metal and base metal. Diffusion at the interface continues with time at elevated temperature and any distinct layer of brazing filler metal will finally disappear. Then the joint properties are nearly the same as those of the base metal.

If a filler metal is used and it does not melt or alloy with the base metal to form a liquid phase, the process is DFW.

The purpose of the filler metal is to aid bonding, particularly during the first stage of DFW. It helps to eliminate voids at the interface that result when two rough surfaces are mated together. By proper selection, the filler metal will soften at welding temperature and flow under pressure to fill the interface voids. Also, it will diffuse with the base metal and produce a joint with acceptable properties for the application. The filler metal is considered to be a *diffusion aid,* not a brazing filler metal.

Principles of Diffusion Welding

For conventional DFW without a diffusion aid, the three stages shown in Fig. 1 adequately describe weld formation. In the first stage, deformation of the contacting asperities occurs primarily by yielding and creep deformation mechanisms to provide intimate contact over a large fraction of the interfacial area. At the end of this stage, the joint is essentially a grain boundary at the areas of contact with voids between these areas. During the second stage,

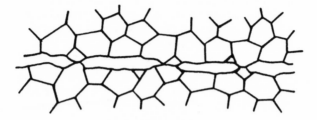

Initial asperity contact

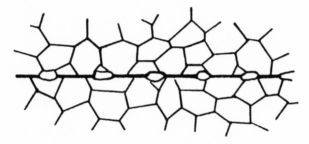

First stage deformation and interfacial boundary formation

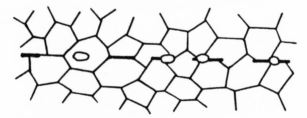

Second stage grain boundary migration and pore elimination

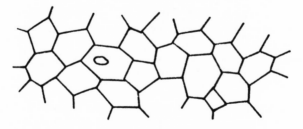

Third stage volume diffusion pore elimination

Fig. 1 – Three-stage mechanistic model of DFW

diffusion becomes more important than deformation and many of the voids disappear as grain boundary diffusion of atoms continues. Simultaneously, the interfacial grain boundary migrates to an equilibrium configuration away from the original plane of the joint, leaving many of the remaining voids within the grains. In the third stage, the remaining voids are eliminated by volume diffusion of atoms to the void surface (equivalent to diffusion of vacancies away from the void). Of course, in a real system, these stages overlap, and mechanisms that dominate one stage also operate to some extent during the other stages.

It can be seen from the preceding that to propose a simple universal model for all types of DFW is very difficult. The mechanism can involve one or any combination of a number of metallurgical and mechanical events. The specific conditions under which a diffusion weld is made, as well as the results desired from the weld, will determine which of the phenomenological events are dominant.

There have been numerous experimentally observed trends that consistently agree with the following:

(1) Temperature is the most influential variable since it determines the extent of contact area during stage one and the rate of diffusion that governs void elimination during the second and third stages of welding.

(2) Pressure is necessary only during the first stage of welding to produce a large area of contact at the joining temperature. Removal of pressure after this stage does not significantly affect joint formation. However, premature removal of pressure before completion of the first stage is detrimental to the process.

(3) Rough initial surface finishes generally adversely affect welding by impeding the first stage and leaving large voids that must be eliminated during the later stages of welding.

(4) The time required to form a joint depends upon the temperature and pressure used; it is not an independent variable.

These stages are not applicable to DFB or hot pressure welding processes where intimate contact is achieved through the use of molten filler metal and extensive (macro) deformation, respectively.

At the same time that intimate contact is being achieved as described above, various intervening films must be disrupted and dispersed so that metallic bonds can form. During initial mating surface contact (stage 1), the films are locally disrupted and metal-to-metal contact begins at places where the surfaces move together under shears.

The subsequent steps in the process involve thermally activated diffusion mechanisms that complete film disruption and intimate metal contact through void elimination (stages 2 and 3).

The barrier film is largely an oxide. Proper cleaning methods reduce the other components of film to negligible levels. Two actions tend to disrupt and disperse the oxide film. The first is solution of the oxide in the metal; the second is spheroidization or agglomeration of the film. Oxide films may be dissolved in titanium, tantalum, columbium, zirconium, and other metals in which interstitial elements are highly soluble. If the oxide is relatively insoluble in the metal, as in the case of aluminum, the disruption action for the trapped film is spheroidization. This leaves a few oxide particles along the weld line. However, if the weld is properly made, these oxide particles are no more detrimental than the inclusions normally present in most metals and alloys.

Both actions require diffusion. Solution occurs by diffusion of interstitial atoms into the metal and spheroidization by diffusion as a result of the excessive surface energy of the thin films. The time for solution of a film of thickness, X, is proportional to X^2/D, where D is the diffusion coefficient. The film must be very thin if DFW times are to be within acceptable limits. Spheroidization occurs more rapidly if the oxide films are thin. Hence, control of the film thickness after cleaning and any increase in thickness during heating to welding temperature are critical factors in DFW.

Once actual metal-to-metal contact is established, the atoms are within the attractive force fields of each other, and a high strength joint is generated. At this time, the joint resembles a grain boundary because the metal lattices on each side of the line have different orientations. However, the joint may differ slightly from an internal grain boundary because it may contain more impurities, inclusions, and voids that will remain in full asperity if deformation has not occurred (stage 2 for achieving intimate contact is not yet complete). As the process is carried to completion, this boundary migrates to a more stable non-planar configuration, and any remaining interfacial voids are eliminated through vacancy diffusion.

An intermediate metal (diffusion aid) is of significant practical importance in many systems, although the mechanisms so far described do not consider its use. When a diffusion aid is used or dissimilar alloys are welded, the additional factor of interdiffusion must be considered to develop a complete understanding of the DFW process.

Key Variables of the Process

Whether the process is DFW or DFB, there are several key variables that in theory must be controlled and in practice are effectively controlled.

Surface Preparation. The surfaces of parts to be diffusion welded or diffusion brazed must be carefully prepared before assembly. Surface preparation involves more than cleanliness. It also includes (1) the generation of an acceptable finish or smoothness, (2) the removal of chemically combined films (oxides), and (3) the cleaning of gaseous, aqueous, or organic surface films. The primary surface finish is obtained ordinarily by machining, abrading, grinding, or polishing.

One property of a correctly prepared surface is flatness. A certain degree of flatness and smoothness is required to assure uniform contact for DFW or uniform joint gap for DFB. Conventional metal cutting, grinding, or abrasive polishing methods are usually adequate to produce needed surface flatness and smoothness. A secondary effect of machining or abrading is the cold work introduced into the surface. Recrystallization of the cold-worked surfaces tends to increase the diffusion rate across the interface between them.

Chemical etching or pickling, commonly used as a form of preweld preparation, has two effects. The first is the removal of nonmetallic surface films, usually oxides. The second is the removal of part or all of the cold-worked layer that forms during machining, if that is done. The need for oxide removal is apparent because it interferes with diffusion.

Degreasing is a universal part of any procedure for surface cleaning. Alcohol, trichlorethylene, acetone, detergents, and many other cleaning agents may be used. Frequently, the recommended degreasing technique is very intricate and may include multiple rinse-wash-etch cycles in several solutions. Since some of these cleaning solvents are toxic, proper safety precautions should be followed when they are used.

Heating in vacuum may also be used to obtain clean surfaces. The usefulness of this method depends to a large extent upon the type of metal and the nature of its surface films. Organic, aqueous, or gaseous adsorbed layers can be easily removed by vacuum heat treatment at elevated temperatures. Most oxides do not dissociate during a vacuum heat treatment. It is possible to dissolve adherent oxides in some base metals at elevated temperature. Typical metals are zirconium, titanium, tantalum, and columbium. Cleaning in vacuum usually requires subsequent vacuum or controlled atmosphere storage and careful handling to avoid the recurrence of surface adsorbed or chemisorbed layers.

Many factors enter into selecting the total surface preparation treatment. In addition to those already mentioned, the specific welding or brazing conditions may affect the selection. With higher temperature or pressure, it becomes less important to obtain extremely clean surfaces. Increased atomic mobility, surface asperity deformation, and solubility for impurity elements all contribute to the dispersion of surface contaminants. As a corollary, with lower temperature or pressure, better prepared and preserved surfaces are an asset.

Preservation of the clean surface is necessary following the surface preparation. One requirement is the effective use of a protective environment during the DFW or DFB cycle. A vacuum environment provides continued protection from contamination. A pure hydrogen atmosphere will minimize the amount of oxide formed and it will reduce existing surface oxides of many metals at elevated temperature. However, it will form hydrides with zirconium, columbium, and tantalum that may be detrimental. Argon, helium, and sometimes nitrogen can be used to protect clean surfaces at elevated temperatures. When these gases are used, their purity must be very high to avoid recontamination. Many of the precautions and principles applicable to brazing atmospheres can be applied directly to DFB or DFW.

Temperature. Temperature is an important DFW process variable for a number of reasons:

(1)   It is readily controlled and measured.

(2)   In any thermally activated process, an incremental change in temperature will cause the greatest change in process kinetics compared to most other process variables.

(3)   Virtually all the mechanisms in DFW are temperature sensitive.

(4)   Elevated temperature, physical and mechanical porperties, critical temperatures, and phase transformations are important reference points in the effective use of DFW.

(5)   Temperature must be controlled to promote or avoid certain metallurgical factors, such as allotropic transformation, recrystallization, and solution of precipitates.

In general, the temperature at which DFW will take place is above 0.5 Tm, where Tm is the melting temperature of the metal. Many metals and alloys can best be diffusion welded at temperatures between 0.6 and 0.8 Tm. For any specific application, temperature, pressure, time at temperature, and surface preparation are interrelated.

Time. Time is closely related to temperature in that most diffusion controlled reactions vary with time. Experience indicates that increasing both time at temperature and pressure increases joint strength up to a point. Beyond this point, no further gains are achieved. This illustrates that time is not a quantitively simple variable. The simple relationship that describes the average distance traveled by an atom does not reflect the more complex changes in structure that result in the formation of a diffusion weld. Although atom motion continues indefinitely, structural changes tend to approach equilibrium. An example of similar behavior is the recrystallization of metals.

In a practical sense, time may vary over an extremely broad range, from seconds to hours. Production factors influence the overall practical time for DFW. An example is the time necessary to provide the heat and pressure. When the system has thermal and mechanical (or hydrostatic) inertia, welding times are long because of the impracticality of suddenly changing the variables. When there are no inertial problems, welding time may be as short as 0.3 min when joining thoria-dispersed nickel to itself. On the other hand, it may be as long as 4 hours when joining columbium with zirconium as a diffusion aid. For economic reasons, the time necessary for DFW should be a minimum for best production rates.

Pressure. Pressure is an important variable. It is more difficult to deal with as a quantitative variable than either temperature or time. Pressure affects several aspects of the process. The initial phase of bond formation is certainly affected by the amount of deformation induced by the pressure applied. This is the most obvious single effect and probably the most frequently and thoroughly considered. Higher pressure invariably produces better joints when the other variables are fixed. The most apparent reason for this effect is the greater interface deformation and asperity breakdown. The greater deformation may also lower recrystallization temperature and accelerate the process of recrystallization at a given temperature.

Practical limitations on pressure are the apparatus available to apply it as well as the joint geometry. The pressure needed to achieve a good weld is closely related to the temperature and time, and there is some range of pressure in which good welds can be made. Pressure has additional significance when dissimilar metal combinations are considered. From economic and manufacturing aspects, low welding pressure is desirable. High pressure requires more costly apparatus, better control, and generally more complex part-handling procedures.

The pressures and temperatures employed are largely interdependent, but the pressure is usually kept slightly below the bulk yield stress at the temperature employed, which itself is selected to produce a weld in an acceptable time.

Metallurgical Factors. In addition to the process variables, there are a number of metallurgically important factors that should be considered. Two factors of particular importance with similar metal welds are allotropic transformation and microstructural factors that tend to modify diffusion rates. Allotropic transformation (or phase transformation) occurs in some metals and alloys. Heat-treatable alloy steels are the most familiar of these, but titanium, zirconium, and cobalt also undergo allotropic transformation. The importance of the transformation is that the metal is very plastic during that time. This tends to permit rapid interface deformation at lower pressures, in much the same manner as does recrystallization. Diffusion rates are generally higher in plastically deformed metals as they recrystallize.

Another means of enhancing diffusion is alloying or, more specifically, introducing elements with high diffusivity into the system at the interface. The function of a high diffusivity element is to accelerate the atomic motion across the interface. In addition to simple diffusion acceleration, the addition of these alloying elements may have secondary effects. The elements should have reasonable solubility in the metal to be joined and depress the melting point locally, but not form stable compounds. Alloying must be controlled to avoid liquefaction at the joint interface.

When using a diffusion-activated system, it is desirable to heat the assembly for some minimum time, either during or after the welding process, to disperse the high diffusivity element away from the interface. If this is not done, the high concentration of the element at the joint may produce metallurgically unstable structures. This is particularly important for joints that will be exposed to elevated temperature service.

Diffusion Aids. It is sometimes advantageous to use some form of diffusion aid or interlayer between the faying surfaces. A soft metal layer permits plastic flow to take place at lower pressures than would be required without it during the first stage of welding. After the joint is formed, the diffusion alloying elements from the base metal into the soft layer reduces the compositional gradient across the joint.

Intermediate diffusion aids may be necessary or advantageous in certain applications to:

(1) Reduce welding temperature

(2) Reduce welding pressure

(3) Reduce process time

(4) Increase diffusivity

(5) Scavenge undesirable elements

Diffusion aids can be applied in many forms. They can be electroplated, evaporated, or sputtered into the surface to be welded, or they can be in the form of foil inserts of powder. The thickness of the interlayer should not exceed 0.010 inch. Generally, the diffusion aid is a more pure version of the base metal being joined. For example, unalloyed titanium often is used as an interlayer with titanium alloys, and nickel is sometimes used with nickel-base superalloys. Silver can be used with aluminum. Diffusion aids containing rapidly diffusing elements also can be used. For example, beryllium can be used with nickel alloys to decrease diffusion time. When selecting a diffusion aid, one should assure that it does not melt at welding temperature or form a low-melting eutectic with the base metal. An improperly chosen diffusion aid can:

(1) Decrease the temperature capability of the joint

(2) Decrease the strength of the joint

(3) Cause microstructural degradation

(4) Result in corrosion problems at the joint

Deformation vs Diffusion Welding

Since DFW is any joining process in which two or more solid phases are "metallurgically joined," the term can be used to describe weld formation by the action of atomic forces rather than solely by mechanical interlocking or by a nonmetallic adhesive. DFW can be divided into two general categories: deformation welding and diffusion welding. Deformation welding includes those techniques in which gross plastic flow that promotes intimate contact and breaks up surface oxides is the principal factor in the formation of a weld and diffusion is not essential. Processes in this category include friction welding (FRW), explosive welding (EXW), high-pressure and roll welding (HPE-ROW) (yield-stress controlled), and forge welding (FOW). In DFW, deformation occurs only on a microscale, and diffusion is the principal factor in the formation of a weld. Included in this group are the following:

(1) Gas pressure welding (isostatic)

(2) Vacuum diffusion welding (creep controlled)

(3) Press or die pressure welding

(4) Transient and eutectic melt

Among the numerous DFW processes is isostatic DFW, also called Thermovac welding. The gas pressure welding process is also known as hot isostatic pressure (HIP) welding. Both processes require an autoclave or other suitable source of gas pressure, and both extract pressure from the gas medium by isolating the joint interface from the gas through the use of a metal can or other method of sealing. In both processes, the internal volume within either the metal can or the welded structure is evacuated prior to the welding step. Hence, the principal difference between Thermovac and HIP is the absence of internal support tooling in the Thermovac method. Thus, unlike the situation during HIP welding, in which the stresses on the structure are ideally all compressive and balanced, the stress state is not in balance in the Thermovac method.

Some of the advantages of the HIP welding process for joining complex shapes are as follows:

(1) Adequate metallurgical bonds can be obtained.

(2) Close dimensional control can be achieved.

(3) Many similar or dissimilar materials can be welded together, usually in a one-step operation.

(4) Components of brittle metals that cannot be joined by conventional techniques can be solid-state welded.

(5) In some cases, fabricated costs can be lower than those for conventional processes.

Another DFW process is roll diffusion welding. The diffusion welded joint between structural details is accomplished by gross plastic flow during hot rolling.

The roll weld process allows flexibility in selecting the structural arrangement and in the fabrication procedure. The process has been applied most frequently to titanium and its alloys.

The press DFW process involves the assembly of premachined and cleaned titanium details in a tooling arrangement designed so that pressure can be applied to all interfaces being joined.

A relatively new process is called continuous seam diffusion bonding (CSDB). This process joins components by "yield-controlled DFW." The parts, such as two flanges and a web, are positioned with tooling and then fed through a machine with four rollers. The top and bottom rollers are made of molybdenum and function much like resistance seam welding wheels. The two side rollers are used to maintain the shape of the components.

The wheel and parts are heated by electrical resistance to the desired temperature. A special control system monitors part temperature. Welding temperature is usually between 1800 and 2000° F for titanium and the 2000 to 2200° F range for nickel-base superalloys. The hot wheels apply pressure in the range of 1 to 20 ksi on the seam. The actual pressure depends upon the metal being joined, the joint design, the temperature, and the welding speed.

The use of intermediate diffusion aids has produced several distinct DFW processes. One is "activated diffusion bonding," which is the name given a joining process for high-strength nickel-base superalloys. This process combines the manufacturing ease of brazing with the high joint strengths achievable by solid-state DFW. This new process basically involves vacuum furnace brazing with an ultra-high-strength bonding alloy (nearly identical in chemical composition to the base metal being joined), followed by diffusion and aging heat treatments to produce maximum joint strength.

The process differs radically from solid-state DFW in that only nominal pressures 0 to 0.01 ksi are required to effect a sound joint. The process is similar to solid-state DFW in that high vacuums, 10^{-3} torr, in leaktight furnaces are an absolute requirement for success and that a subsequent heat treatment is necessary to develop maximum joint mechanical properties. The low pressure used in this process allows it to be used for joining relatively fragile parts of complex configuration without risking deformation during joining.

Transient liquid phase (TLP) is another new DFW process used for producing diffusion bonds in nickel-base and cobalt-base heat-resistant alloys. Because pressure requirements during welding are extremely low (0.01 ksi), complex shaped parts can be joined economically without the need for elaborate tooling or bonding presses. Boron was found to be a key additive to the interlayer material because of its effectiveness as a melting point depressant and because of its rapid diffusivity during postbond heat treatment. The boron content is controlled in the interlayers to obtain an optimum balance between melting point and ease of subsequent homogenization.

Several DFW processes have been developed for titanium and its alloys. One of these processes forms a metallurgical joint between the titanium surfaces with the aid of a thin film of a series of electroplated elements. Upon the application of heat and a pressure sufficient to maintain contact between the surfaces, the intermediate film forms a transient molten phase with the titanium surfaces being joined. The intermediate alloy is then diluted in the base metal by thermal diffusion.

Two process variations take advantage of the superplastic properties of certain metals or alloys. The alloys can deform or flow significantly at elevated temperatures under very small applied loads without necking or fracture. Titanium and its alloys exhibit this superplastic behavior in the temperature range of 1400 to 1700° F. Complex shapes can be formed using moderate gas pressures, and then the shapes can be diffusion welded together, or vice versa.

One of these process variations is called creep isostatic pressing (CRISP). It is a two-step process combining creep or superplastic forming of titanium sheet structures with hot isostatic pressing to produce a diffusion welded one-piece structure. Inherent in the CRISP process is the mating of two external skins. This is accomplished through a combination of creep forming and isostatic DFW to produce a structure. First, one skin is creep-formed by gas pressure to the contour of a die. Then, shaped inserts are positioned in place and a second skin is creep-formed by gas pressure over the first skin and inserts. Assembly of the formed sheets and inserts by DFW is achieved by hot isostatic pressing in an autoclave. This method eliminates the need for precision machined die sets and close dimensional tolerances in parts.

The second process variation utilizes the same properties of titanium and its alloys described previously; however, the welding is performed under low-pressure conditions. This variation is known as "superplastic forming/ diffusion bonding" (SPF/DB). It is a two-stage process in which titanium is joined without melting. Since superplastic forming and DFW of selected titanium alloys can be accomplished using identical process temperatures, the two operations can be combined in a single fabrication cycle. However, welding must be accomplished under low-pressure conditions.

The superplastic forming of the sheet can be done first followed by welding, or it can be done in reverse. The order depends on the design of the component. Forming is done first, if this is required, to bring the faying surfaces of the joint together for welding. If the faying surfaces are in contact, welding is done first, and then the part is formed to shape in the die using inert gas pressure. A suitable nonmetallic agent can be used to prevent welding where subsequent forming is to occur.

Equipment and Tooling

A wide variety of equipment and tooling is employed in DFW activities. The only basic requirement is that pressure and temperature must be applied and maintained in a controlled environment. Various types of equipment have been developed, each with its special advantages and disadvantages. There are numerous variations of a given type of equipment or approach depending upon the specific application. A general description of four types of DFW equipment follows.

Isostatic Gas Pressure. The pressure for welding can be applied uniformly to all joints in an assembly using gas pressure. One important requirement is that the assembly to be welded be evacuated of air during the welding cycle. The assembly itself may be evacuated and sealed by fusion welding if this is possible. Otherwise, it must be sealed in a thin gas-tight envelope that is evacuated and sealed.

The primary component of hot isostatic equipment is a cold wall autoclave, which can be designed for gas pressures up to 150 ksi and for part temperature in excess of 3000° F. Internal water cooling is usually provided to maintain a low wall temperature. Closures on each end provide access to the vessel cavity. Utilities and instrumentation are brought into the vessel through high-pressure fittings located in the end closures. The high temperatures are produced with an internal heater. Resistance heaters of various designs are employed. Alumina or silica insulation is used to reduce heat losses to the cold wall. Temperature is monitored and controlled by thermocouples located throughout the furnace and vessel. Pressurization is achieved by pumping inert gas into the autoclave with a multiple-stage piston type compressor. Control of temperature and pressure are independent and any combination of heating and pressurizing rates can be programmed. The autoclave is a pressure vessel, and it must be designed to meet applicable code requirements.

The most important consideration is the gas-tight envelope or can in which the specimen must be contained. If a leak develops in the can, pressure cannot be applied to or maintained on the joint. Sufficient gas pressure is applied so that local plastic flow will occur at the joint interface and all void space will be filled by diffusion. With proper conditions, essentially no deformation occurs and no change in part dimensions will occur during the operation.

The chief advantage of this technique is its ability to handle complex geometries. It is also well suited to batch operations where large quantities of relatively small assemblies can be processed simultaneously. The major drawbacks are the capital equipment costs and the size limitations imposed by the internal dimensions of the autoclave. Operational equipment ranges up to 36 in. inside diameter and inside lengths of up to 108 inches.

The gas pressure process variables are not uniform for different metals and combinations of metals. Usually, joints are made at the highest possible pressure to minimize the temperature needed. This method is well suited for welding brittle metals or metals to ceramics and cermets because the isostatic pressure eliminates tensile stresses in the materials.

Presses. A very common approach for DFW employs a mechanical or hydraulic press of some design. The basic requirements for the press are (1) sufficient load and size capacity, (2) an available means for heating, and (3) the maintenance of uniform pressure for the required time. It is often necessary to provide a protective atmosphere chamber around the weldment. Press equipment that can be adapted to DFW applications is frequently available in the manufacturing or development organization.

There is no standard press design. Some units provide a vacuum or an inert atmosphere around the parts. Radiant, induction, and self-resistance types of heating are used. An advantage of a press setup is the ease of operation and the excellent process control available. A disadvantage is the practical limitation of press size when considering large component fabrication. This approach does not lend itself to high production rates and rapid turnaround or batch operations.

Some of the limitations on size can be overcome by operating in large forming or forging press without an inert atmosphere chamber. Heated platens are used to apply both heat and pressure to the components. The platens may be metallic or ceramic depending upon the temperature and pressure employed. Castable ceramics are particularly useful because contours can easily be accommodated without extensive machining. Heating elements can be cast into a ceramic die to provide uniform heat during welding. Close tolerances must be maintained between the die and the part so that uniform pressure will be applied to the joint. This is a major problem with press type equipment. It is extremely difficult to maintain uniform pressure on the joint, and variations in weld quality can result.

Tooling requirements vary with application. If no lateral restraint is provided, upsetting may occur during the welding cycle. In such cases, lower pressure or temperature is usually required. Heated dies are required because of the time factor and die materials can be a problem. The die must be able to withstand both the temperature and pressure and be compatible with the metal to be welded. Interaction between the part and the die can be controlled by stopoff agents and sometimes by oxidizing the die surface. Atmosphere protection is often achieved by sealing the parts in evacuated metal cans that are designed to conform to the die shape.

Retorts can be used in conjunction with presses for DFW of titanium parts. Tooling blocks and spacers of Type 22-4-9 stainless steel may be used to fill any voids between the titanium pieces to maintain their shapes. Presses with side and end restraining jacks can exert up to 2 ksi pressure on the retort in all directions. In actual production, the completed assembly pack, (retort, heating pads, and insulation) is preheated before it is placed in the press. Large structures may require a preheat for as long as 40 hours. Several packs may be in assembly and preheat at one time. The actual time in the press will vary from 2 to 12 hours, depending upon the shape of the structure and the mass of titanium. The assembly pack is cooled to room temperature, dismantled, and the retort is then cut open. This approach is quite slow and may not be scaled readily to high production rates.

Resistance Welding Machines. Resistance welding equipment may be used to produce round diffusion spot welds between sheet metal parts. In general, modification of standard equipment is not necessary to achieve successful diffusion welds. The interface is resistance heated under pressure with this equipment. The cycle is designed to avoid melting of metal at the interface. Weld times are generally less than 1 second.

As in standard resistance welding, selection of a suitable electrode material is important. The electrodes must be electrical conductors, possess high strength at welding temperatures, be thermal shock resistant, and resist sticking to the parts. There is no universal electrode material because of potential interaction with the workpiece. Each system must be carefully evaluated from a metallurgical compatibility standpoint.

For some applications, a small chamber surrounding the electrodes is used to provide an inert atmosphere or vacuum during welding.

One advantage of this type of equipment is the speed at which diffusion welds can be made. Each weld is made in a very short time. However, only a small area is welded in each cycle and a number of welds are needed to join a large area.

Tooling. A number of important considerations must be observed in the selection of tooling materials. The main criteria are:

(1) Ease of operation

(2) Reproducibility of the welding cycle

(3) Operational maintenance

(4) Weld cycle time

(5) Initial cost of tooling

Furthermore, the materials must be capable of maintaining their proper position and shape throughout the heating cycle.

Suitable fixture materials may be limited when welding temperatures are above 2500° F. Only the refractory metals and certain nonmetallic materials have sufficient creep strength at high temperatures. For example, tantalum and graphite may be suitable for fixturing tungsten. Ceramic materials are suitable for fixtures provided they are completely outgassed prior to welding.

Since pressure is required for DFW, fixtures should be designed to take advantage of the difference in thermal expansion between the metals being joined and the fixture material. It is possible to generate at least part, if not all, of the pressure required for welding by appropriate selection of the fixture material and the clearances between the fixture and part. These principles have been used to join Type 2219 aluminum alloy tubing to Type 321 stainless steel. A precise method was devised to apply the correct welding pressure to a tubular assembly. Tooling was developed that provides a uniform and reproducible welding pressure by taking advantage of the difference in the thermal expansions of low alloy steel and stainless steel.

Diffusion Brazing Principles

Diffusion brazing (DFB) produces joint properties that are significantly different from those of conventional brazed joints. The main objective of the process is to produce joints having mechanical properties approaching those of the base metal in:

(1) Alloys that are not weldable for their intended application, such as cast nickel-base superalloys for high temperature service and beryllium alloys

(2) Dissimilar alloy combinations that are not weldable

(3) Alloys where a combination joining and heat-treating cycle is desirable to minimize distortion of the assembly during processing

(4) Alloys where conventional brazed joint properties are too low for the intended application, particularly at elevated temperatures (as in the application of high strength titanium alloys in aircraft)

(5) Large complicated assemblies where it is economical to produce many strong joints simultaneously and conventional brazing is unsuitable

Two approaches to DFB are used. One utilizes a brazing filler metal that has a chemical composition approximately the same as the base metal but with a lower melting temperature. Melting temperature is suppressed by adding certain alloying elements to the base metal composition or to a similar alloy composition. For example, the melting temperature of a nickel-base high-temperature alloy can be lowered by a small addition of silicon or boron. In this case, the brazing filler metal melts and wets the base metal faying surfaces during the brazing cycle. This approach is sometimes called activated diffusion bonding (ADB) or transient liquid phase bonding (TLP).

The other approach is to braze with a metal that will alloy with the base metal to form one or more eutectic compositions. When the brazing temperature is slightly higher than the eutectic temperature, the filler metal and base metal will alloy together to produce a eutectic composition. The filler metal itself does not melt but alloy (eutectic) is formed *in situ*. The method is also known as eutectic bonding or liquid interface diffusion (LID). An example is the DFB of titanium alloys with copper.

With either approach, the assembly is held at temperature for a sufficient time for diffusion to produce a nearly uniform alloy composition across the joint. As this takes place, the melting temperature and strength of the joint increase. The processing time depends upon the degree of homogeneity desired, the thickness of the initial filler metal layer, and the temperature. Heating rate to brazing temperature may also be important. A low heating rate will allow more solid-state diffusion to take place, and more filler metal will be required to provide sufficient liquid to fill the joint. Conversely, if a large quantity of filler metal and fast heating are used, the molten metal may run out of the joint and erode the base metal. The thick joint so formed will require a longer diffusion time to achieve a suitable composition gradient across it.

The composition gradient across the joint may be important with respect to response to subsequent heat treatment. This is particularly true for metals that undergo phase transformation during heating and cooling. Alloy composition will determine the transformation temperature and rate of transformation. Therefore, the phase morphology and mechanical properties of the joint can be controlled by the joint design and the brazing cycle.

Key Process Variables. DFB operations are similar to those for conventional brazing. Methods of heating, atmospheres, joint designs, and equipment can generally be used interchangeably. With DFB, the brazing filler metal, processing temperature, and time at temperature are selected to produce a joint with physical and mechanical properties almost identical to those of the base metal. To do this, it is necessary to essentially eradicate the braze layer by diffusion with the base metal.

Temperature and Heating Rate. The temperature cycle used for DFB depends upon the base metal, and since the design of the brazing filler metal composition is similar to that of the base metal, the assembly must be heated to the melting temperature of the brazing filler metal as in conventional brazing. As the brazing melts, it wets the base metal and fills the voids in the joint. Then the temperature is reduced to solidify the brazing filler metal.

Some DFB systems form a filler metal *in situ* during the brazing cycle. The systems are generally designed to form a molten eutectic that flows and fills the voids in the joint at brazing temperature. The brazing temperature is somewhat higher than the eutectic temperature. For example, a plating of copper on a silver base metal faying surface will form a eutectic when heated to 1500° F. The eutectic melting temperature is 1435° F.

In systems where several eutectic and peritectic reactions take place at different temperatures, both the brazing temperature and the heating rate are important. Although a liquid phase can form at the lowest eutectic temperature, diffusion rates will be faster at higher temperatures. Heating rate will determine whether or not a molten eutectic is formed. If the heating rate is too low, solid-state diffusion will prevent the formation of a molten eutectic. The voids at the faying surface will not be filled with "filler metal." An example of this type of system is the use of a copper interlayer with titanium or zirconium alloys.

The maximum brazing temperature may be established by the characteristics of the base metal (incipient melting in some nickel-base alloys, for example). It may also be limited by the effect of temperature on the final metallurgical structure and by the heat treatment requirements for the weldment.

After brazing is accomplished, the part temperature may be reduced to solidify the brazing layer. Temperature is then maintained while solid-state diffusion takes place.

Time. The duration of the DFB cycle will depend upon (1) the brazing temperature, (2) the diffusion rates between the filler metal and the base metal at temperature, and (3) the maximum concentration of interlayer metal permissible at the joint. The alloy composition at the joint may influence the response to heat treatment and the resulting mechanical properties of the joint. Therefore, the joint must be held at temperature for some minimum time to reduce the concentration of interlayer metal to an acceptable value.

Pressure. Normally, brazing is done with very little or no pressure on the joint. In some cases, fixturing may be necessary to avoid excessive pressure. This is particularly so when the molten filler metal is to flow into the joint by capillary action. When the filler metal is preplaced in the joint, excessive pressure may force low melting constituents to flow out of the joint before brazing temperature is achieved. In that case, the molten filler metal may not be sufficiently fluid to fill interface voids.

Metallurgical Factors. The metallurgical events that may occur during DFB are similar to those with DFW. An additional factor is the variation in alloy content across the joint. It is well known that compositional variations can significantly affect the response of a particular alloy to heat treatment. With metals that experience an allotropic transformation at elevated temperature, alloying can raise or lower the transformation temperature and the rate of transformation. Thus, the response to heat treatment across a diffusion brazed joint may vary with the concentration of the metal used to lower the melting temperature of the base metal. For example, copper stabilizes the beta phase in titanium and decreases the beta-to-alpha transition temperature.

Intermediate Metals. The intermediate material may be either a brazing filler metal or a metal that will alloy with the base metal at some elevated temperature to form a brazing filler metal. In the latter case, a eutectic must form the melt at a temperature compatible with the metallurgy and design properties of the base metal. The metal or alloy may be in powder, foil, or wire form, or it may be plated onto the surface of the base metal. Close control of the amount of metal or alloy in the joint is essential for consistent joint properties in production.

Pure metals and simple alloys may be electroplated or vapor deposited on the joint faces. However, these processes are not economical for all cases. Preformed metal foil or wire shapes are better suited for many applications.

In the case of nickel and cobalt-base heat-resisting alloys, elements commonly added to depress the melting temperature increase embrittlement. Consequently, they can only be produced in powder form. This presents a problem in DFB where precise amounts of filler metal are required. Boron in the range of 2.0 to 3.5 percent is used in nickel-base brazing filler metals. This element can be diffused into the surfaces of nickel alloy foil or wire shapes to produce brazing filler metal placement for DFB applications.

Equipment and Tooling. The equipment and tooling used for DFB is essentially the same as that used for conventional brazing. If furnace brazing is used, the entire cycle can be done in the same equipment. In some cases, it may be more economical and convenient to braze in one piece of equipment and then follow with a diffusion heat treatment in another piece of equipment. For example, the brazing could be done with resistance welding or induction heating equipment, and the diffusion heat treatment performed in a furnace.

DFW and DFB Advantages and Limitations

DFW and DFB have a number of advantages and limitations in comparison to the more commonly used welding processes and conventional brazing.

Some of the advantages of the two processes are as follows:

(1) Joints can be produced with properties and microstructures very similar to those of the base metal. This is particularly important for lightweight fabrications.

(2) Components can be joined with minimum distortion and without subsequent machining or forming.

(3) Dissimilar alloys can be joined that are not weldable by fusion processes or by processes requiring axial symmetry.

(4) A large number of joints in an assembly can be made simultaneously.

(5) Components with limited access to the joints can be assembled by these processes.

(6) Large components of metals that require extensive preheat for fusion welding can be joined by these processes. An example is thick sections of copper.

(7) Defects normally associated with fusion welding are not encountered.

Each specific DFW or DFB process has its own economical advantages and limitations.

One of the chief advantages of press welding is the relatively inexpensive equipment required. Conventional hydraulic presses can supply the required welding pressures. Welding temperatures can be provided by a wide range of methods including resistance, induction, and radiant heaters, or simply by heating with an oxyacetylene torch. Also, since many pressure welding operations can be carried out in air, additional equipment to provide protective atmospheres is not required in many applications.

Depending upon the equipment available and the characteristics of the materials to be joined, welding time can be very short, sometimes on the order of seconds. Another advantage of the process is that the finish of joint surfaces is not very critical. However, deformation is common with pressure welding, and if subsequent machining to remove this deformation is required, joint surface preparation may reduce cost savings.

Transient-melt DFW has a very significant advantage in that low welding pressures are always used. However, there are two important limitations: Prolonged diffusion treatment is required to eliminate joint remelt temperatures, and the high diffusivity of the liquid phase accelerates tendencies for void formation that can result from interdiffusion of dissimilar metals in the weld area.

The chief limitations of gas pressure welding stem from the high cost of the equipment it requires and the limited size of the workpiece that current equipment can handle. Because of high equipment costs, conventional joints by gas pressure welding are more expensive than those of other DFW processes. In addition, because of the slow heat-up characteristics of autoclaves, welding cycle times are usually 3 hours and more.

The roll DFW process can be performed on conventional rolling mills, and the only restriction on the size of the structure that can be produced is the capacity of the rolling mill. The range of materials that can be joined by roll welding is broad. However, the limitation exists that high-temperature, high-strength materials may require roll pressures not possible with conventional equipment, and expensive modification of conventional rolling facilities may be required.

Redesign may be necessary to achieve maximum cost-effectiveness. A wing beam was designed to be manufactured by machining from plate or from a forging. Stepwise thickness changes in web and caps were used to facilitate machining. Redesign was possible with uniform thickness throughout most of the web and a continuous taper in the caps. It will be noted that in the design for machining, provision was made for access for the cutter leads to a nonoptimum cap configuration that tapers to its extremity. A more efficient design with uniform thickness caps was possible by DFW from constant-thickness or simple tapered sheets. In this example, cost-effectiveness results from the following:

(1) Metal recovery increase from less than 10 percent to greater than 90 percent of the raw material.

(2) Less than 5 percent of the final part surface is generated by machining, in contrast to 100 percent in the original design.

(3) More effective cap shape is possible with DFW.

In conclusion, DFW can be an extremely effective means to reduce costs and increase part effectiveness. The process will require appreciation by the designer of the requirements for effective fabrication by DFW, generation of design data for use by the structural analyst, demonstration of producibility and reproducibility by the manufacturing engineer, and development of acceptance criteria and inspection methods by quality control engineers.

Materials

A wide variety of similar and dissimilar material combinations can be successfully joined by DFW and DFB. Most applications involve alloys of titanium, nickel, and aluminum, as well as dissimilar metal combinations. The ability to produce joint properties approaching those of the base metal depends largely upon the characteristics of the metals being joined. For example, excellent joint properties are readily produced in titanium alloys. The relatively low creep strength of titanium alloys and their ability to dissolve the oxide at the elevated temperature contribute to this.

On the other hand, nickel-base heat-resistant alloys are difficult to join, particularly in the solid state, because their creep strengths are high, requiring high pressures for DFW, and chromium oxides are stable at high temperatures. In addition, unless a proper interlayer metal is utilized, stable intermetallic precipitates can form at the interface and produce brittle joints.

The ability to achieve a joint with base metal properties depends upon the mechanism used to develop the design strength of the base metal, cold work or heat treatment. If cold work is used, then the strength of the base metal will be irreversibly lowered by either process. On the other hand, heat-treatable alloys can generally be strengthened with a thermal treatment combined with or subsequent to the joining operation.

Beryllium and Its Alloys. Beryllium's high strength-to-weight ratio and low neutron-absorption cross section make it especially interesting for aircraft and nuclear applications. Its usage, however, has been limited because of the difficulty of joining or fabricating this characteristically brittle metal into desired shapes without extensive machining. Cold-worked beryllium can be diffusion welded by holding it at temperatures of 1500 to 1650° F and pressures of about 10 ksi for 4 hours. In general, mechanical cleaning, followed by wiping with acetone or ether, constitutes good surface preparation for beryllium. It also can be prepared by grinding with wet silicon carbide paper and polishing with alumina in dilute oxalic acid. On the other hand, Be-38Al alloy can be diffusion welded without special surface preparation.

Beryllium-copper (Cu-1.7Be) is readily diffusion welded. Joint tensile strengths average 108 ksi, or well over twice that of brazed beryllium-copper joints. Good welds are obtained with a minimum pressure (about 0.006 ksi) by using a silver-indium-copper diffusion aid. Using either a hydrogen atmosphere or a vacuum, the weld cycle is approximately 30 min at 1475 to 1550° F.

Nickel and Its Alloys. Many nickel alloys, specifically the high-strength, heat-resistant alloys, are more difficult to solid-state diffusion weld than most other metals. These alloys must be welded at temperatures close to their melting temperatures and with relatively high pressures because of their high-temperature strengths. In addition, extra care must be taken in preparing the surfaces to be welded to ensure mutual conformity and cleanliness. Surface oxides that form on these alloys are stable at high temperatures and will not dissolve or diffuse into the alloy. During the welding operation, the ambient atmosphere must be carefully controlled to prevent interface contamination.

Pure nickel or nickel alloy interlayers, typically an electroplated layer or thin foil, are commonly used when diffusion welding nickel alloys. These interlayers, generally from 0.0001 to 0.001 in. thick, serve several functions. Their relatively low yield strength allows surface conformity to take place at relatively low welding pressures. More important, they are used during welding to prevent the formation of stable precipitates, such as oxides, carbides, or carbonitrides, at the joint interface. The DFW time must be adequate to allow sufficient interdiffusion to occur in the joint region.

Some nickel-base heat-resistant alloys that have been diffusion welded with the welding conditions are listed in Table 1.

Table 1
Typical DFW variables for some nickel-base alloys

Alloy	Interlayer	Welding temp (°F)	Pressure (psi)	Time (hr)
Inco 600	Ni	2000	100-500	1/2
Hastelloy X	Ni (.0004 in.)	2050	100-500	4
Wrought U-700	Ni-35% Co (.0002 in.)	2140	1000	4
Cast U-700	Ni-35% Co (.0002 in.)	2175	1200	4
Rene 41	Ni-Be	2150	1550	2
Mar M-200	Ni-25% Co	2200	1000-2000	2

The pressure required for satisfactory welding is influenced strongly by the geometry of the parts being welded. Therefore, the required pressure for each application must be determined empirically.

The significance of an interlayer and its composition was demonstrated by a series of diffusion welds in wrought and cast Udimet 700 alloy. Welds were made without an interlayer and with 0.0002 in. interlayers of both pure nickel and Ni-35% Co alloy. The welding conditions were the same as those listed for this alloy in Table 1.

Nickel-base heat-resistant alloys can be diffusion brazed using specially designed brazing filler metals and procedures. There are two reported variations that differ primarily in the manner of programming the thermal cycle to accomplish diffusion. Both utilize specially tailored interlayers that melt at brazing temperature. Then through diffusion, either by extending the original thermal cycle or with a subsequent cycle, both methods produce high-strength joints that resemble the base metal in both structure and mechanical properties.

With the first variation, a thin interlayer alloy, 0.001 to 0.004 in. thick, of specific composition and melting point is used as brazing filler metal. The parts are held together under slight compressive pressure (under 10 psi) and heated to the brazing temperature (typically 2000 to 2200° F) in vacuum or in an argon atmosphere. At brazing temperature, the interlayer initially melts, filling the voids between the mating surfaces with a thin molten layer. While the parts are held at temperature, rapid diffusion of alloying elements occurs between the interlayer and the base metal. This change of composition at the interface region causes the joint to isothermally solidify, thus forming a solid bond while still at temperature. After isothermal solidification occurs, the joint microstructure generally resembles that of the base metal except for some compositional and structural variations.

At this stage the joint has good properties, although they are not fully equivalent to those of the base metal. By permitting the part to remain at the brazing temperature for longer times, the joint can be homogenized both in composition and structure until it is essentially equivalent to the base metal.

The second variation involves joining nickel-base components with a specially designed brazing filler metal that completely melts at some elevated temperature below the incipient melting point of the alloy or alloys being joined. Subsequent to this, the brazed component is given a diffusion heat treatment to affect homogenization of the brazing filler metal and the base metal. This is followed by an appropriate aging heat treatment designed for the base metal.

Melting point depressants, such as silicon, boron, manganese, aluminum, titanium, and columbium are added to the base alloy to produce a brazing filler metal. The base alloy is simply "doped" with sufficient amounts of depressants so that the resultant alloy is molten at a temperature that does not impair the properties of the alloy to be joined. Ideally, brazing is accomplished at the normal solution heat-treating temperature for a given alloy.

A diffusion brazed joint in wrought Udimet 700 was made using an interlayer of 0.003 in. thick Ni-15% Cr-15% Co-5% Mo-3% B filler metal in the joint with a processing cycle of 2140° F for 24 hours in vacuum. A microprobe chemical analysis across a joint showed a uniform chemical composition, essentially that of the base metal. Stress rupture tests at 1600° F and 1800° F showed that diffusion brazed joints had essentially the same properties as the Udimet 700 base metal.

Diffusion brazed joints produced at lower temperatures and shorter time cycles may not be uniform in composition. As a result, some elevated temperature mechanical properties of the joints may be lower than those of the base metal, particularly under stress-rupture conditions.

Titanium and Its Alloys. Many potential DFW and DFB applications involve titanium alloy components, the majority of which are Ti-6% Al-4% V alloy. The popularity of the processes with titanium alloys stems from the following factors:

(1) Titanium is readily joined by both methods without special surface preparation or unusual process controls.

(2) Diffusion welded or brazed joints may have better properties for some applications than conventional fusion welded joints.

(3) Most titanium structures or components are used principally in aerospace applications where weight savings are more important, within limits, than manufacturing costs.

A number of well established DFW and DFB methods are available for joining titanium alloys. Welding can be accomplished using pressures in the range of several hundred to several thousand psi. High pressures are used in conjunction with low welding temperatures and when the assembly is welded in a closed container (retort). Inserts may be used to hold the structure to dimensions. When welding at higher temperatures without an enclosure, maximum pressure is usually limited by the allowable deformation in the parts, and this pressure must be determined empirically. Pressures of 300 to 500 psi work well in many cases. In some applications, total assembly deformation and deformation rate, rather than pressure per se, are controlled during welding or process control.

Welding temperature is probably the most influential variable in determining weld quality and is set as high as possible without causing irreversible damage to the base metal. For the commonly used alpha-beta type titanium alloys, this temperature is about 75 to 100° F below the beta transus temperature. For example, Ti-6% Al-4% V alloy with a beta transus of approximately 1825° F is best diffusion welded between 1700 and 1750° F. The time required to achieve high weld strength can vary considerably with other factors, such as mating surface roughness, welding temperature, and pressure. Welding times of 30 to 60 minutes should be considered a practical minimum, with 2 to 4 hours being more desirable. Mating surface finish and preweld cleaning procedure are two other important considerations. Although the general rule that a smooth mating surface makes welding easier applies, parts with relatively rough (milled or lathe-turned) mating surfaces can be successfully diffusion welded as long as welding temperature, time, and pressure are adjusted to accommodate such rough finishes. Freshly machined mating surfaces only need to be degreased with a suitable solvent prior to welding. Hydrocarbon and chlorinated solvents should not be used. A preferred cleaning method is acid cleaning in a HNO_3-HF solution. Any residue remaining from the cleaning operation must be removed by thorough rinsing.

Several industries, the aircraft industry in particular, have taken advantage of the benefits of the DFW process with the increased potential usage of titanium alloys. Two new vehicles, one for space travel and a long range bomber aircraft, are utilizing this process extensively. The engine mount of each Space Shuttle vehicle will have 28 diffusion welded titanium parts, from large frames to interconnecting box tubes. This structure is capable of withstanding three million pounds of thrust. Square tubes of 0.75 in. thick wall and approximately 8 in. long sides were fabricated by DFW in lengths up to 180 inches.

The advanced airplane has 66 diffusion welded parts of Ti-6% Al-4% V alloy. The wing carry-through structure, the most critical structure in the vehicle, is the largest diffusion welded composite structure in existence.

A helicopter rotor hub has been successfully produced by DFW in a press.

CSDB has been used to produce stiffened skins fabricated as an integral one-piece structure. One of the first applications for this method was the fabrication of curved Ti-6% Al-4% V alloy I-beams used as structural members to support a boron-aluminum composite on a fighter airplane. These beams were made from 0.025 in. sheet.

DFB techniques are also used for joining titanium alloys. Cycle times, temperatures, and preweld cleaning procedures are much the same as for DFW. However, pressure just sufficient to hold the parts in contact is needed, and mating surface finish requirements are not stringent.

The mating surfaces are electrolytically plated with a thin film of either pure copper or a series of elements, such as copper and nickel. When heated to the brazing temperature of 1650 to $1700°$ F, the copper layer reacts with the titanium alloy to form a molten eutectic at the joint interface. The assembly is then held at temperature for at least 1.5 hours, or given a subsequent heat treatment at this temperature for several hours, to reduce the composition gradient in the joint. Diffusion brazed joints made with a copper interlayer and a cycle of $17°$ F for 4 hours had tensile, shear, smooth fatigue, and stress corrosion properties equal to those of the base metal. However, they had slightly lower notch fatigue and corrosion fatigue properties, and significantly lower fracture toughness. A Widmanstatten structure normally is formed at the joint because the plated interlayer stabilizes the beta phase of the titanium alloy.

DFB is being used to fabricate lightweight cylindrical cases of titanium alloys for jet engines. In this application, the titanium core is plated with a very thin layer of selected metals that react with the titanium to form a eutectic. During the brazing cycle in a vacuum of 10^{-5} torr, a eutectic liquid forms at $1650°$ F. This liquid performs the function of a brazing filler metal between the core and face sheets. The eutectic quickly solidifies due to rapid diffusion at the joints. The assemblies are held at temperature for one to four hours to reduce the composition gradient at the joint by diffusion.

Aluminum and Its Alloys. Aluminum alloys can be successfully diffusion welded as long as some means is employed to avoid, disrupt, or dissolve its tenacious surface oxide. Although a wide range of temperatures, pressures, and times may be utilized, the main boundary condition is the melting point of the specific alloy being joined. For example, Type 6061 with aluminum alloy welding conditions as divergent as $725°$ F and a pressure of 3800 psi for several hours, or $1000°$ F and a pressure of 1000 psi for 1 hour, have been satisfactory. The welding operation is normally carried out in vacuum or inert gas although aluminum-boron fiber composites can be diffusion welded in air. For applications where little or no local deformation of the parts can be tolerated, the mating surfaces are first coated with a thin layer of silver or gold-copper alloy by electrolytic or vapor deposition. The coating prevents surface oxidation during welding.

Aluminum and aluminum-silicon alloys can be diffusion brazed using a copper interlayer. Sound, strong joints can be produced in aluminum by limiting the copper thickness to 20 microns and restricting the brazing temperature to between 1030 and $1060°$ F. The time at temperature should not exceed 15 minutes at the lower temperature limit or 7 minutes at the upper limit. Type A356.0 aluminum-7% silicon casting alloy can be diffusion brazed by electroplating one of the joint members with copper that will form a eutectic with the aluminum and silicon in the casting alloy when heated to $975°$ F.

To ensure optimum joint properties, the copper thickness, brazing temperature, and time-at-temperature must be selected to promote isothermal solidification during brazing and thereby prevent the formation of the compound $CuAl_2$. Proper balancing of these variables results in strong joints that can withstand quenching from above the solution treating temperature, which is required for heat-treating Type A356.0 alloy to the T61 condition. Electroplating the cover sheets with 150 to 200 microinches of copper and holding between 980 and $1000°$ F for one hour are satisfactory conditions. After quenching and aging, the joint strength will equal that of the casting itself. Microstructurally, the brazed joint will be indistinguishable from the casting.

Steels. Steels are not normally diffusion welded because, for most applications, they are more easily joined by conventional brazing or fusion welding methods. DFW may be utilized successfully for specialized applications where high quality joints are required between large flat surfaces. For example, plain carbon steels have been welded without an interlayer over a wide range of conditions. Two sets of variables that produced excellent welds in AISI 1020 steel are 1800 to $2200°$ F with a pressure of 1 ksi for 1 to 15 minutes, and 2000 to $2200°$ F with a pressure of 5 psi for 2 hours. Welding can be accomplished either in a protective atmosphere or in air, provided the joint is first seal welded around the periphery to exclude air.

Stainless steels can be diffusion welded using conditions similar to those used for plain carbon steel. However, these steels are normally covered by a thin adherent oxide that must be removed prior to welding. This can be accomplished either by welding at high temperatures in dry hydrogen or by copper plating the faying surfaces after anodic cleaning. Copper oxide on the plating is relatively easy to reduce in hydrogen during heating to welding temperature. For illustrative purposes, sound welds were made in AMS 5630 martensitic stainless steel at 2000° F with a pressure of 100 psi for 1.5 hours using a 0.0001 in. thick copper interlayer.

Refractory Metals and Their Alloys. HIP welds in Cb and Cb-V alloys have been successfully made at 2400° F with a pressure of 10 ksi for 3 hours in vacuum. Columbium alloy Cb-752 (10W-2.5Zr-Rem Cb) has been successfully diffusion welded by blanket and resistance heating methods. A diffusion aid of 0.002-in. titanium foil with a DFW cycle of 2200° F at 1×10^{-6} torr for 6 hours was used to produce the components (honeycomb sandwich) with the electric blanket method. Utilizing resistance heat, the cycle entailed 2100° F at 1 ksi for 15 minutes. The atmosphere protecting the parts for both methods was argon.

Columbium alloy D-36 (10Ti-5Zr-Rem Cb) has been diffusion welded by resistance and induction heating methods. Diffusion aids of vanadium, tantalum, and columbium foil have been used successfully to join the alloy, and self-welding has been used as well. All systems produced welds, but the self-weld condition gave the highest joint strengths and the vanadium foil provided a good alternative system. Although surface preparation was found to be not critical when an intermediate material was used, an abraded and degreased surface was optimum in the self-welding of this alloy.

Columbium alloy B-66 (5Mo-5V-1Zr-Rem Cb) has been successfully diffusion welded by induction heat both in the self-weld condition and with a 0.003-in. tantalum intermediate foil. Columbium, tantalum, and vanadium foils have also been used as intermediates in the resistance DFW of B-66 alloy. The optimum surface preparation for DFW B-66 alloy with an intermediate foil was degreasing in a salt solution. This preparation produced the highest strength lap joints. One last Cb alloy, D-43 (10W-1Zr-0.1C-Rem Cb), has been diffusion welded by induction heating, and high peel strengths have been obtained in the self-welded condition and with vanadium and tantalum intermediates.

Several DFW techniques have been applied to joint molybdenum and its alloys with a fair amount of success (see Table 2).

Pure tantalum has been diffusion welded successfully by HIP at 2350° F with 10 ksi pressure in 2.5 hours. An intermediate diffusion aid, zirconium, has produced excellent joints at temperatures as low as 1600° F, well below the normal recrystallization temperatures.

Table 2
Variables

Material	DFW process	Temperature	Pressure	Time	Comments
Pure molybdenum	Hot isostatic	2600° F	10 ksi	3 h	HIP welds produced were of high quality with complete grain growth across the original weld interface. HIP produced loss of ductility, but 25% cold rolling restored ductility.
	Vacuum hot press	1840° F	30 ksi	1 h	0.001 in. columbium foil has been successfully used as a diffusion aid to produce excellent welded joints below the recrystallization temperature of molybdenum.
	Induction heating with and without intermediate diffusion aids	2012° F	5 ksi	15 min	Diffusion welds without an intermediate aid were produced at higher temperatures than the recrystallization temperature of pure molybdenum with 5 to 10% deformation, but the joints made at higher temperatures than 2192° F were brittle because of recrystallization. Grain growth across the interface was observed to occur at 2282° F for 5 min and migration of grain boundaries took place easily at relatively low temperatures. It was also found that the formation of the molybdenum joint without recrystallization and large deformation was accomplished with an intermediate aid such as iron, nickel, copper, or silver prepared by electroplating. The remelting temperature of the joint was much higher than the melting one of the intermediate aid. Although nickel formed an intermetallic compound with molybdenum, the nickel intermediate aid made a stronger joint at low temperatures than the others. Copper was also found to be applicable as an intermediate aid, but

Table 2
Variables (cont'd)

Material	DFW process	Temperature	Pressure	Time	Comments
Molybdenum-0.5Ti	HIP	2600° F	10 ksi	3 h	
	Resistance heating	2100° F	0.5 ksi	15 min	
	Vacuum hot press	1680° F	For titanium, 30 ksi	20 min	Titanium and nickel 0.001-in. foils as diffusion aids. The shear strength of the joint with titanium was 20.7 ksi while the nickel joint produced 33.8 ksi.
		1700° F	For nickel, 30 ksi	20 min	
TZM (0.5Ti-0.1 Zr-Rem Mo)	Induction heating	2200° F	10 ksi	1 min	Columbium, tantalum, and vanadium 0.001-in. foils as diffusion aids. The tantalum yielded the highest room temperature shear strength, 0.7 ksi.

Resistance heating of the 90Ta-10W alloy has produced diffusion welds in 15 min at 2500° F and 0.5 ksi in an argon atmosphere. The tantalum alloy T-111 (8W-2Hf-Rem Ta) has been resistance and induction diffusion welded with and without any aids. The most successful system has used a 0.003-in. tantalum foil at 2600° F at 24 ksi for 20 seconds.

HIP welding of tungsten has been accomplished at 2800° F and 10 ksi for 3 hours. Vacuum hot press DFW has been successful on tungsten, and for sustained high-temperature application, either a tungsten-titanium or a tungsten-columbium intermediate system has produced minimum diffusion activity.

Dissimilar Metal Combinations. DFW is particularly well suited for joining many dissimilar metal combinations, especially when the melting points of the two metals differ widely or when the materials are not metallurgically compatible. In such cases, conventional fusion welding is not practical because it would result either in excessive melting of one of the metals or formation of a brittle weld metal. DFW is also suitable when the high temperatures of fusion welding would cause an alloy to become brittle or lower its strength drastically, as is the case with some refractory metal alloys. Interlayer metals are sometimes used to prevent the formation of brittle intermetallic phases between certain metal combinations.

When determining conditions and interlayer requirements for diffusion welding a particular dissimilar metal combination, the effects of interdiffusion between the two metals must be considered. Interdiffusion can cause certain problems as a result of the following metallurgical phenomena:

(1)   Intermediate phase or brittle intermetallic compound formation at the interface. Selection of an appropriate interlayer can usually prevent problems associated with this effect.

(2)   Low melting eutectic phase formation. This effect can be used to advantage in some applications.

(3)   Joint porosity due to dissimilar rates of metal transfer by diffusion in the region adjacent to the weld interface (Kirkendall porosity). Proper welding conditions or use of an appropriate interlayer, or both, may prevent this problem.

One often existing problem is the difference in thermal characteristics of the two metals. This is not unique to DFW. Simply stated, any combination of dissimilar metals that are heated and cooled during welding or brazing will develop shear stresses in the joint if their thermal expansion characteristics are not identical. The severity of the problem will vary depending upon the temperature, the net difference between the rates of expansion, the size and shape of the parts, and the nature of the bond formed between them. This becomes a design problem, in part, since distortion can result. The most severe difficulty is cracking through the joint in cases where the bond strength or ductility, or both, are low and the shear stresses are high.

Some representative conditions used for diffusion welding some dissimilar metal and nonmetal combinations are presented in Table 3. Often the temperature and time used for a particular combination are selected as part of the necessary heat treatment for one of the alloys to develop design properties for the application.

Applications — Current and Future

Many industries have taken advantage of the benefits of DFW and DFB.

Dimensionally, press diffusion welded parts probably are limited only by the length and breadth of press beds. Future DFW consideration is being given to main landing gear beams for commercial airlines, which now are fabricated from extrusions and sheet metal parts with mechanical fasteners. Future consideration will also be given to a new process — diffusion weld riveting.

The press DFW process has been successful in producing helicopter rotor blade spares of Ti-6Al-4V alloy. The laminated hub required a 4500-ton press and only 64 lbs of metal had to be removed after DFW. This new approach could remove one of the main limits in fabricating rotor hubs for heavy-lift helicopters.

The three most recently developed DFW processes are being utilized by design engineers who are continually finding aircraft uses. Sandwich honeycomb structures of 6AL-4V and Ti-6-2-4-2 have been diffusion welded with plated diffusion aid materials. These structures are being used in engine applications.

The second process of note is CSDB. The process is exemplified by a tee-stiffened skin fabricated as an integral one-piece structure, which is typical of aircraft designs.

The third process is SPF/DB. The use of this process is gaining momentum not only from industry but also from government-sponsored programs. One of the largest parts to be diffusion welded will be an engine nozzle fairing.

The joining specialist and the engine designer have found that several DFW processes are quite amenable to weight and cost reductions in current and future high-thrust engines. These include CSDB, HIP, and intermediate diffusion aids. An aircraft turbine engine fan blade of Ti-6Al-4V alloy was locally stiffened by DFW with an inlay of Ti-6Al-4V/50B composite in recesses in the blade surface. Various dynamic tests, including engine tests, of blades resulted in no failures at the composite inlay. The advantage of the composite inlay, in this case, was a significant improvement in blade vibration stability because of the high elastic modulus of the composite.

With HIP, diffusion welds have been achieved in the fabrication of rotors from AISI 4340 and Inconel 718.

Table 3
Dissimilar metal and nonmetal combinations

Materials joined	Temperature	Time	Pressure	Intermediate layer	Method used
Titanium to stainless steel	500 to 1600° F	30 min	5.5 to 30 ksi	Silver plate	Vacuum furnace or argon atmosphere
Beryllium to stainless steel	1450° F	2 hr	Differential thermal expansion	Silver plate	Vacuum
Mo-.5Ti to st. stl. and F-48 to st. stl.	1800 to 2000° F	4 hr	Threaded screw	None	Vacuum
Cb-1Zr to st. stl.	1800° F	4 hr	Differential thermal expansion	Cb-1 Zr	
Alum. to st. stl.	500 to 600° F	2 to 4 hr	20 to 25 ksi	Silver plate	Vacuum
Bronze to st. stl.	580° F	15 to 20 min	25 ksi	Copper	Furnace and flux
Alum. to titanium	500° F	2 hr	Differential thermal expansion	Silver plate	Air
Beryllium to titanium	1570° F	—	.64 ksi	Silver plate	Vacuum
Titanium to copper	1760 to 1796° F	5 hr	.28 to .5 ksi	Columbium foil	Vacuum
Graphite to refractory metals	1634 to 1841° F	5 to 10 min	0.04 to .1 ksi	Titanium foil plated with copper	Vacuum
Columbium to ceramics	2200 to 2300° F	3 hr	10 ksi	Chromium	Vacuum
Ceramics (Al_2O_3) to st. stl., kovar, titanium, nichrome, low alloy steel, and palladium.	2282 to 2372° F	10 min	0.01 ksi	None	Vacuum

Blades, vanes, and disks are important components of engines, and with the use of diffusion aid materials, considerable advances have been and will be achieved in joining Udimet 700, Ti-6Al-4V and Ti-6Al-2Sn-4Zr-6Mo, Rene 80, TD-NiCr, and B1900.

One of the first applications for the CSDB process was for curved Ti-6Al-4V I beams used as structural members supporting boron-aluminum composite on a fighter airplane. These beams were made from 0.025-in. Ti-6Al-4V sheet. The alternate method of fabrication was machining from 1-in. plate stock; material savings with CSDB exceeded 90 percent.

Other I beams have been produced from 0.070-in. Ti-6Al-4V sheet and tested in a reverse bending mode. The results demonstrated a fatigue life exceeding 10^7 cycles at flange stresses of 83 ksi, and all failures originated at the edges of the flanges, well away from the diffusion welds. Sections are currently produced by machining extrusions that are 0.25 to 0.35-in. thick and more than 70 percent of the metal is machined away.

Two companies have recently described their production of hollow titanium rotor blade spars. A 4000 lb titanium alloy billet is forged and extruded into a 3400 lb hollow tube, then machined and creep formed. The companies have been able to apply the CSDB process to such spares; 120 in. lengths were made from 0.125-in. Ti-6Al-4V sheet with a diffusion welded butt joint. Preliminary fatigue results on this spar were encouraging and show that DFW offers an approach that will markedly improve metal recovery, will offer a high performance product, and will reduce cost.

Closed structures are also possible with CSDB. A typical engine strut was fabricated from 0.063-in. Ti-6Al-4V. The part was made by welding two vee-gutters to the median stiffening rib. Removable, reusable internal tooling supported all three members and provided surfaces against which fillet radii were formed.

A more complex hollow strut is the inlet guide vane for a new engine being developed in Europe. Through prototype production of this vane by CSDB and structural evaluation, it has been demonstrated that significant cost reduction and improved performance can be achieved over vanes made by fusion welding. Six vanes have been fabricated from 0.070-in. Ti-2.5Cu alloy sheet by CSDB. Each vane was made by joining six sheet metal components. First, tee-joint welds were made to join the ribs to the two outer skins. Then lap type joints were made to weld a filler strip into the leading and trailing edges. Removable internal tooling was used to produce controlled radii at all joints.

Another example of a hollow sheet metal part made by CSDB is the vanes for an advanced new engine. These vanes were made by joining two preformed skins of 0.035-in. Ti-6Al-4V along the leading and trailing edges. The vane performance was excellent in engine tests. Multiple tee-joints can be combined in a single part to make rib stiffened panels. The panels can be flat or curved, and the tooling is reusable. A Ti-6Al-4V panel, 36-in. in length and stiffened by five ribs, has been applied to structures in a variety of metals including mild, stainless, and precipitation-hardening steels; superalloys; zirconium; and refractory metals. In general, the process is not ideally suited to aluminum, although very satisfactory aluminum-to-steel joints have been made.

A tee-joint in Hastelloy X that forms the support members for the open-face honeycomb-core turbine seals on a commercial aircraft engine has been made. These seals are segmented. The tee beams are made in straight 120-in. lengths by diffusion welding a 0.095-in. stem to a 0.045-in. thick cap. For turbine seals, CSDB has replaced machined ring forgings, reducing cost while increasing metal recovery by a very significant amount. Approximately 40,000 feet of tee section has been made for this application. Other applications include gas-cooled walls in jet engine combustors and cooled walls for pressure vessels.

Other industries are starting to utilize DFW. Columbium wires in a copper-tin alloy matrix is a prime example of new generation composite superconductors developed through the use of diffusion welds to form the superconductive phase *in situ.* A flat cable connecting system that terminates wires by DFW is now being marketed. The machine puts terminals on 800 wires per hour, or 100 contacts at a time. Furthermore, users of the system no longer have to strip insulation or crimp the connection. The machine will handle closely spaced terminals, as close as 0.050 inch. A short pulse of heat from the machine vaporizes and gets rid of the wire insulation while joining the wire to the terminal connector. Diffusion and grain growth form a weld of greater tensile strength and electrical continuity than crimping, soldering, and fusion welding.

The general areas of current and future applications are:

(1) Large area overlap joints

(2) High strength-to-weight ratio structures

(3) Heat exchangers

(4) Composite structures
    (a) Filled composites
    (b) Laminar composites
    (c) Cellular composites
    (d) Metal/ceramic composites

(5) Hybrid structures

(6) Complex forgings

Finally, as little as 6 years ago the application of DFW to large-scale structures and components, except in very special cases, was a mere possibility on a far horizon. Developments in the intervening period have revealed the true potential of these techniques, and general large-scale application is an exciting prospect for the forthcoming decade.

The transformation has been from a process for unusual materials to a process for ordinary materials, and from a process for the small component to one for major structural assemblies.

The ability of DFW to produce high-quality joints in all types of material has been long known, but now its competitive potential in relation to conventional fusion welding processes has been revealed.

The difficulties associated with future development center upon joint assessment and the mechanical aspects of equipment construction, but both can be readily overcome.

Bibliography

Albom, M.J. 1964. Solid-state bonding. *Weld. J.* 43(6): 491.

Angerman, C.L. 1961. Metallographic studies of Al-Ni-U bonds in nuclear fuel elements. *ASME Trans. Quart.* 54(3): 260-275.

Arata, Y.; Shima, K.; Terai, K.; and Nagai, Y. 1972. The forecasting of welding processes in the future by the Delphi method. *Trans. Jpn. Weld. Soc.* 3(1); and *Weld. Res. Abroad* 19(7): 14-40.

Auleta, J.J.; Finch, D.B.; Goodman, L.; Lew, D.E.; Mandel, H.; and Rubenstein, H.J. 1963. Piqua nuclear power facility operations analysis program, Prog. Rep. 2, Fiscal Year 1963. *USAEC Rep. NAA-SR-8722*, Atomics International.

Bangs, J. January 1976. Diffusion bonding: no longer a mysterious process. *Weld. Des. Fabr.* pp. 43-46.

Bartle, P.M. and Ellis, C.R.G. 1969. Diffusion bonding and friction welding, two newer processes for the dissimilar metal joint. *Met. Constr. Brit. Weld. J.* 1(12s): 88-95.

Bartle, P.M. 1969. Introduction to diffusion bonding. *Met. Constr. Br. Weld. J.* 1(5); and *Weld. Res. Abroad.* 15(9): 33-36.

Bartle, P.M. 1975. Diffusion bonding: a look at the future. *Weld. J.* 54(11): 799-804.

Baskey, R.H. 1960. Fuel-bearing fiberglass in aluminum-base fuel elements. *USAEC Reps. ORO-303* (June 13, 1960); *ORO-304* (July 7, 1960); *ORO-316* (Sept. 2, 1960); and *ORO-322*, Clevite Corp.

Bondarev, V.V. 1967. On the problem of brazing graphite and some other materials. *Weld. Prod. (USSR)* 14(6): 17-19.

Bosworth, T.J. 1972. Diffusion welding of beryllium: part 1 — basic studies. *Weld. J.* 51(2): 579s-590s.

Bosworth, T.J. 1973. Diffusion welding of beryllium: part II — the role of the microalloying elements. *Weld. J.* 52(1): 38s-48s.

Brick, R.M. 1970. Hot roll bonding of steel. *Weld. J.* 49(9): 440s-444s.

Brunken, R.D. et al. 1973. Manufacturing methods for roll diffusion bonded stiffened skin structure. *AFML-TR-72-169*, Contr. F33615-69-C-1877.

Bryant, W.A. 1975. A method for specifying hot isostatic pressure welding parameters. *Weld. J.* 54(12): 433s-435s.

Carlson, C.E.; Delgrasso, E.J.; and Varholak, E.M. 1969. Mechanical properties of braze bonded borsic^{TM}-aluminum composites. *15th SAMPE Nat. Meeting,* Los Angeles.

Castle, C.H.; Melnyk, P.; and West, W.G. 1972. Process development for boron-aluminum fan blades. *Tech. Memo TM-4663* TRW, Cleveland.

Cogan, R.M. and Shamblem, C.E. 1969. Development of a manufacturing process for fabricated diffusion bonded hollow blades. *Rep. AFML-TR-69-219,* Contr. F33615-68-C-1215, General Electric Com., Cincinnati.

Crane, C.; Lovell, D.; and Baginski, W. *Research study for development of techniques for joining of dissimilar metals. NAS 8-11307,* DCNI-4-50-01068-01 (IF).

Crane, C.H.; Torgerson, R.T.; Lovell, D.T.; and Baginski, W.A. 1966. Study of dissimilar metal joining by solid-state bonding. *NASA Contr. NAS 8-20156.*

Crane, C.H.; Lovell, D.T.; and Johnson, H.A. 1967. Study of dissimilar metal joining by solid-state welding. *NASE Contr. NAS 8-20156.* (Amendment No. 2).

Diersing, R.J.; Hanes, H.D.; and Hodge, E.S. 1963. Fabrication of beryllium-clad tubular hypervelocity impact targets by gas-pressure bonding. *NAS 3-3651,* Summary Rep., NASA Cr-54058, Battelle Memorial Institute, Columbus, OH.

Diersing, R.J.; Carmichael, D.C.; Hanes, H.D.; and Hodge, E.S. 1965. Gas-pressure bonding of stainless steel-reinforced beryllium hypervelocity impact targets. *Rep. NASA CR-54173,* Contr. NAS 3-5139, Battelle Memorial Institute, Columbus, OH.

Dring, M.L. 1963. Ceramic-to-metal seals for high-temperature thermionic converters. *Tech. Doc. Rep. TDR-63-4109,* Contr. AF33(657)-10038, Red Bank Division, Bendix Corp., Eatontown, NJ.

Duvall, D.S.; Owczarski, W.A.; Paulonis, D.F.; and King, W.H. 1972. Methods for diffusion welding the superalloy Udimet 700. *Weld. J.* 51(2): 41s-49s.

Duvall, D.S. and Owczarski, W.A. 1973. Fabrication and repair of titanium engine components by welding. *5th Nat. SAMPE Tech. Conf.* vol. 5, pp. 472-485.

Duvall, D.S.; Owczarski, W.A.; and Paulonis, D.F. 1974. TLP* bonding: a new method for joining heat resistant alloys. *Weld. J.* 53(4): 203-214.

Feduska, W. and Horigan, W.L. 1962. *Welding Journal* 41(1): 28-35.

Francis, W.C. and Craig, S.E. 1970. Progress report on fuel-element development and associated projects. *USAEC Rep. ID0-16574,* Phillips Petroleum Co.

Freedman, A.H. 1971. Basic properties of thin-film diffusion brazed joints in Ti-6Al-4V. *Weld. J.* 50(8): 356s-434s.

Freedman, A.H. 1972. Nor-Ti-bond. AWS, San Francisco.

Gerken, J.W. and Owczarski, W. *TRW Rep. ER 6563* June 23, 1965.

Hamilton, C.H. 1975. Diffusion bonding on the B1 aircraft. *ASM Conf. - Joining Titanium for Aerospace Applications.*

Hamilton, C.H.; Stacher, G.W.; and Li, H.W. *Manufacturing methods for SPF/DB process.* IR-798-5 (I through VIII), January 1975 to January 1977, AFML Contr. F33615-75-C-5058.

Hashimoto, T. and Tanuma, K. 1970. Diffusion welding of molybdenium. *Trans. Nat. Res. Inst. Met.* 11(5): 1969; and *Welding Res. Abd.* 26(7): 2-10.

Hersh, M.S. 1973. Resistance diffusion bonding boron/aluminum composite to titanium. *Weld. J.* 52(8): 370s-376s.

Holko, K.H. 1972. Hot press and roll welding of titanium-6% aluminum-4% vanadium bar and sheet with auto-vacuum cleaning. *NASA TND-6958.*

Holko, K.H. and Moore, T.J. 1972. Enhanced diffusion welding of TD-NiCr sheet. *Weld. J.* 51(2): 81s-89s.

Holko, K.H. 1973. An improved diffusion welding technique for TD-NiCr sheet. *Weld. J.* 52(11): 515s-523s.

Hoppin, G.S. III, and Berry, T.F. 1970. Activated diffusion bonding. *Weld. J.* 49(11): 505s-509s.

Houck, J.A. and Bartlett, E.S. 1967. The roll-diffusion bonding of structural shapes and panels. *DMIC Rep. S-17* pp. 1-37.

Kaufman, A.; Berry, T.F.; and Meiners, K.E. 1971. Joining techniques for fabrication of composite air-cooled turbine blades and vanes. *ASME 71-GT-32* pp. 1-9.

Kazakov, N.F. 1968. Diffusion welding in a vacuum, *Moska, Izdvo, Mashionostroyniye* pp. 1-332.

Kazakov, N.F.; Samoilov, V.S.; and Polyakova, M.L. 1972. Vacuum diffusion bonding of VK20 hard alloy to steel. *Svar. Proizvod.* 2: pp. 18-19; and IIW Doc. IV-127-73.

Kazakov, N.F. et al. Vacuum diffusion bonding of L62 brass for type AMts alloy via a nickel interlayer. *Svar. Proizvod.* 10: 15-16; and IIW Doc. IV-128-73.

Kendall, E.G., et al. 1961. Fabrication development of APM alloys for fuel elements. *USAEC Rep. NAA-SR-6213,* Atomics International.

Kennedy, J.R. 1972. Fusion welding of titanium-tungsten and titanium-graphite composites. *Weld. J.* 51(5): 250s-259s.

Kharchenko, G.K. 1969. Problems in diffusion welding of dissimilar metals. *Avtom Svarka* 22(4): 193.

King, W.H. and Owczarski, W.A. 1968. Additional studies on the diffusion welding of titanium. *Weld. J.* 47(10): 444s-450s.

Lessman, G.G. and Bryant, W.A. 1972. Complex rotor fabrication by hot isostatic pressure welding. *Weld. J.* 51(2): 606s-614s.

Lloyd, H. and Davies, J.M. 1964. Roll bonding of nuclear fuel plates. *British Rep. AERE-R-4634.*

Lucas, J.J. and Doyle, P.J. 1975. Diffusion bonding Ti-6Al-4V helicopter rotor hub and blade spare development. *ASM Conf. - Joining Titanium for Aerospace Applications,* Contracts DAAG46-72-C-0175 and DAAG-46-73-C-0126.

Makara, A.M. and Nazarchuk, A. 1969. The mechanism of diffusion welding and the improvement of the quality of diffusion welds. *Avtom Svarka* 22(4): 193.

Martin, D.C. and Miller, F.R. 1972. Using solid-state joining in gas turbine engines. *ASME 72-GT-74* pp. 1-16.

Materials Engr., pp. 12-13. July 1971. Joining diffusion bonding with forging lowers cost.

Meiners, K.E. 1973. Diffusion bonding of specialty structures. *5th Nat. SAMPE Tech. Conf.* vol. 5, pp. 703-712.

Metcalfe, A.G. and Rose, F.K. 1968. Production tool for diffusion bonding. *Rep. AFML-TR-68-213,* vol. 1, Contr. AF 33(615)-2304.

Metelkin, J.J.; Makarkin, A.Y.; and Pavlova, M.A. 1967. Welding ceramic materials to metals. *Weld. Prod. (USSR)* 14(6): 10-12.

Metzger, G.E. 1975. Joining of metal-matrix fiber-reinforced composite materials. *Weldg. Res. Council Interpretive Rep. 207.*

Miska, K.H. 1976. Diffusion welding joins similar to dissimilar metals. *Mat. Eng.* pp. 18-20.

Mohamed, H.A. and Washburn, J. 1975. Mechanism of solid-state pressure welding. *Weld. J.* 54(9): 210s-302s.

Moore, T.J. and Holko, K.H. 1970. Solid-state welding of TD-nickel bar. *Weld. J.* 49(9): 395s-409s.

Moore, T.J. and Holko, K.H. 1972. Practical method for diffusion welding of steel plate in air. *Weld. J.* 51(3): 106s-116s.

Moore, T.J. 1974. Solid-state and fusion resistance spot welding of TD-NiCr sheet. *Weld. J.* 53(1): 37s-48s.

Morin, T.J.; Whitehead, R.J.; and Zotos, J. 1968. Hydrodynamic welding of steel tubes to ferrous and nonferrous alloys. *ASF Trans.* 76: 515-520.

Morin, T.J. December 1974. Speedy solid-state joining. *Weld. Eng.* pp. 15-16.

NASA, SP-4557. Supersonic cruise aircraft research structural panel program, 8th Semiannual Rep.; Nov. 1, 1976.

Nessler, C.G. 1971. Joining techniques for fabrication of high-temperature superalloy blades. *AFML-TR-71-237*, Contr. F33615-70-C-1784.

O'Brien, M.; Rice, C.R.; and Olson, D.L. 1976. High strength diffusion welding of silver coated base metals. *Weld. J.* 55(1): 25-27.

Ozelton, M.W. et al. 1970. Reactive bonding of solution treated titanium alloys. *AFML-TR-70-23*, Air Force Contr. F33615-69C-1908.

Parks, J.M. 1953. *Weld. J.* 32(5): 209-222.

Patenaude, C.J. and Santschi, W.H. 1964. Casting of beryllium-stainless steel and beryllium-columbium impact target composites. *NASA Contr. NAS 3-3729*, Summary Rep., Beryllium Corp., Reading, PA.

Peaslee, R.L. 1976. Diffusion brazing. *Weld. J.* 55(8): 695-696.

Perun, K.R. 1967. Diffusion welding and brazing of titanium 6Al-4V process development. *Weld. J.* 46(9): 385s-390s.

Porembka, S.W. 1963. Nonglassy phase ceramic-metal bonding. *Final Rep.*, Battelle Memorial Institute, Columbus, OH.

Rajala, R. *Manufacturing methods for low cost non-rotating titanium engine components.* IR-875-5 (IV) (v), October 1975 to March, 1976, AFML Contr. F33615-75-C-5079.

Schneider, G. 1961. Metallic bonding between uranium and aluminum for reactor fuel elements. *Metallurgy* 15(7): 675-679.

Schneider, G. 1964. Leak-tight joints in the fabrication of nuclear fuel elements. *Deutsche Luft und Raum-Fahrt Rep. 64-07,* Deutscher Verlag für Schweiss-Technik (DVS) GMGH, Dusseldorf, West Germany.

Schwartz, M. 1972. LID bonding. Golden Gate Weld. Conf., San Francisco.

Schwartz, M. 1976. Rohrbond. *SME* AD76-280.

Shmakov, V.M. and Izmirlieva, A.N. 1966. Diffusion welding of titanium to bronze. *Weld. Prod. (USSR)* 13(1): 14-17.

Signes, E.G. 1968. Diffusion welding of steel in air. *Weld. J.* 47(12): 51s-57s.

Steel Dec. 2, 1968, pp. 66-67. Diffusion bonding on verge of wider market.

Stocker, B.P.W. 1972. Full-scale fatigue test of a diffusion bonded helicopter main rotor hub. *AFML-TR-72-63*, Contr. F33615-70-C-1327.

Thorsrud, E.C.; Rose, F.K.; and Metcalfe, A.G. October 1974. Improved metal recovery by the CSDB process, *SAE 740835* pp. 1-10.

Tylecote, R.G. and Wynne, E.J. 1963. *Br. Weld. J.* 10(8): 385-394.

Tylecote, R.F. 1967. Diffusion bonding. *Weld. Met. Fabr.* 35(12): 483-489.

Vaidyanath, L.R.; Nicholas, M.G.; and Milner, D.R. 1959. *Br. Weld. J.* 6(1).

Watson, R.D. 1965. Diffusionless bonding of aluminum to zircaloy-2. *Rep. AECL-2243,* Atomic Energy of Canada, Ltd.

Weisert, E.D. and Stacher, G.W. 1977. Fabricating titanium parts with SPF/DB process. *Met. Prog.* pp. 32-37.

Wells, R.R. 1976. Microstructural control of thin-film diffusion brazed titanium. *Weld. J.* 55(1): 20s-28s.

Wiesner, P. Diffusion welding in the G.D.R. *Doc. IV-174-75* Zentralinstitut fur Schweisstechnik der DDR, Halle (Saale).

Wilford, C.F. and Tylecote, R.F. 1960. *Br. Weld. J.* 7(12): 708-712.

Wolf, J.E. 1969. Fabrication techniques for shrouded titanium impeller. *Final Rep. NASA CR-102589.* Contr. NAS 8-20761, Rocketdyne Division, North American Rockwell Corp., Canoga Park, CA. (N70-23376).

Woodward, J. 1973. Titanium honeycomb sandwich fabrication process. *5th Nat. SAMPE Tech. Conf.* Vol. 5, pp. 432-437.

Wu, K.C. 1971. Resistance Nor-Ti-bond joining of titanium shapes. *Weld. J.* 50(9): 386s-393s.

Young, W.R. and Jones, E.S. 1963. Joining of refractory metals by brazing and diffusion bonding. *Tech. Documentary Rep. ASD-TDR-63-88,* Contr. AF33(616)-7484.

Zanner, F.J. and Fisher, R.W. 1975. Diffusion welding of commercial bronze to a titanium alloy. *Weld. J.* 54(4): 105s-112s.

Novel Approaches to Electron Beam Welding Machine Utilization

Frank S. Pogorzelski
McDonnell Aircraft Company

Introduction

At McDonnell Aircraft Company, a division of McDonnell Douglas Corporation, electron beam welding (EBW) has been a production welding process for the past 16 years. Principal applications are in fabrication of aircraft titanium structural components, which would be very difficult or costly to fabricate without welding. Most applications of EBW at McDonnell Aircraft involve a high degree of complexity and have required novel and unique solutions to fabrication problems, and for increased productivity. A few of these applications are described in this paper.

Electron Beam Welding Equipment

Two Sciaky 30 kV electron beam welding machines are currently used for production welding operations (see Fig. 1). Both machines have vacuum chambers that are 62 inches high x 50 inches deep x 112 inches long. Only one has wire feed capability incorporated. The machines are equipped with:

(1)   Head and tailstock

(2)   Rotary table

(3)   Y-axis table

(4)   Reflectron seam scanner

(5)   Small universal head and tailstock (one only)

(6)   Eccentric table (one only)

Most of these accessories are versatile in their capabilities, which are well known. There are applications, however, that require other unique and novel approaches to EB welding machine utilization for profitable production.

EB Welding of F-15 Pylon Posts

The McDonnell Douglas F-15 aircraft's (see Fig. 2) external armament and fuel tanks are attached to pylon assemblies, which are carried under the wings and center fuselage of the aircraft. A major detail of the pylon assembly is the pylon post, which is a light-weight, but highly stressed component fabricated from annealed Ti-6Al-4V die forgings. The pylon posts have a cruciform configuration (see Fig. 3). The posts are fabricated by machining two mating pieces, EB welding the butt joints, and then, finish machining.

41

There are five weld joints in the post including a tapered thickness joint in the upper portion of the post. Each joint is welded with a 100 percent penetration first pass followed by a smoothing or cosmetic weld second pass.

Fig. 1 — Front loading 30 kV EB welding machine

Fig. 2 — McDonnell Douglas F-15 Eagle

Fig. 3 − Ti-6Al-4V pylon posts

To prepare the pylon post for EBW, the two pieces are gas tungsten arc tack welded together in an argon gas-purged manual welding chamber. The pylon post then is clamped to a swivel-based trunnion fixture in the EB weld chamber (see Fig. 4). Using indexing controllers and synchronous motors, the pylon post is indexed into position and the weld joint is aligned paralleled to the EB gun X-axis travel. Solenoid operated shields are used to protect the vacuum chamber light bulbs from metal vapor deposit during the welding operation. This ensures having light available for the positioning of each joint and permits complete welding of a pylon post in one chamber vacuum pump-down.

A relatively inexpensive approach that resulted in a controlled and repeatable operation was applied to produce the 100 percent penetration first weld pass in the tapered thickness butt joint. With the EB welding machine in the diode mode, a Data-Trak chart programmer was set up with a plot of the high voltage required versus position along the length of the tapered joint (see Fig. 5). The programmer is coupled to the power-stat of the machine so that the welding power is increased automatically to the proper value as the EB gun traverses from the thin to the thick section of the joint.

Fig. 4 — Swivel-based trunnion fixture

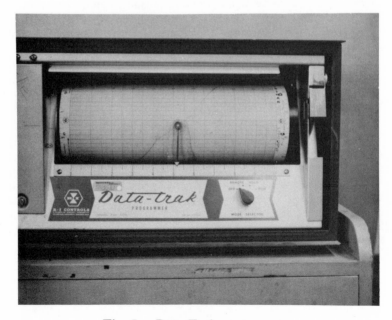

Fig. 5 — Data-Trak programmer

To complete the welding operation, a smoothing or cosmetic weld pass is made on the root bead of all welds. The weld run-on and run-off tabs that were incorporated are removed during the final machining of the pylon post (see Fig. 6). Finally, it is interesting to note that a weld shrinkage of about .020 inches occurs at the cruciform intersection and a corresponding allowance must be made in the machined half-parts. This shrinkage is attributed to a concentration of shrinkage stresses caused by the complex cruciform configuration.

Fig. 6 — Completed pylon post

Electron beam welding of F-15 wing skin "kick rib"

The lower inboard wing skin panels (forward and aft) for the F-15 are designed with integral upstanding stiffener ribs and are each machined from a solid plate of Ti-6Al-4V (see Fig. 7). The inboard-to-outboard ribs are approximately one inch high, making the total panel thickness at these rib sections approximately 1-1/2 inches. However, there is also a single forward-to-aft rib incorporated at the wing station line where the skin is later hot-formed into a downward "kick." This "kick rib" is approximately two inches high, which significantly increases the thickness of raw titanium plate stock and the amount of machining required. Therefore, only a stub root of this kick rib is machined into the skin panel and a rib extension is EB welded to the stub. Thus, the raw material thickness and machining costs are reduced significantly.

Fig. 7 — Lower inboard forward wing skin

To enclose the wing skin welding setup in the EBW chamber, a 68-inch deep chamber extension mounted on air pads was designed and fabricated by Sciaky. It mates with the existing chamber (see Fig. 8). Two men move and position the chamber extension, which weighs 25,000 pounds. The rib extension is clamped, in a weld fixture, to the portion of the rib machined into the wing skin. The weld fixture is pinned on location to a Y-axis table. This entire setup is moved to and from the EBW machine on an air pad-supported transportation table.

The rib extension-to-skin weld joint is at an angle to the face of the rib, to provide access for the electron beam (see Fig. 9). An auxiliary X-axis travel beam was installed in the weld chamber to support and position the EB gun for welding the joint. It incorporates limited Z-axis travel, angular electron beam gun positioning, and angular position locking capabilities.

To facilitate EB gun alignment, small Ti-6Al-4V step blocks are gas tungsten arc tack welded to each end of the rib. The face of the step on the block is located at the intersection of the back face of the rib and weld joint interface. A 3/64-inch diameter hole is then drilled into the face of the step. The hole centerline is at the joint interface. Aligning the hole in the step block and the joint on the face of the rib, by using the Sciaky Reflectron Scanner, positions the EB gun for welding.

Fig. 8 – EBW machine with chamber extension

Wing skin electron beam welding fixture

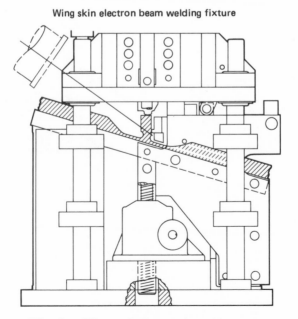

Fig. 9 – View of rib-to-wing skin setup

Welding parameters were developed, and full length test parts clamped in production weld fixtures were EB welded. The weld quality was certified acceptable by our Quality Assurance Division. The first nine production welded wing skins, however, were rejected due to incomplete fusion of the joint near the root bead side. An investigation was immediately started to determine the cause. Two things were suspected: (1) bending or refraction of the electron beam from a straight line as a result of the beam striking the face of the rib at an angle, or (2) misalignment of the beam to the joint.

To test for beam refraction, the EB gun was aligned with the joint interface using the reflectron scanner, exercising normal procedure. The EB gun was locked into the angular position. The gun then was moved vertically to a point approximately one-fourth of an inch above the weld joint. Traveling only along the X-axis, two welds were made in the rib extension. One weld was made with a very sharp focus and the other with the same focus as in the certified EBW machine settings. Cross section of these welds conclusively revealed no bending or refraction of the electron beam had occurred as a result of angular beam impingement on the surface (see weld beam refraction tests in Fig. 10).

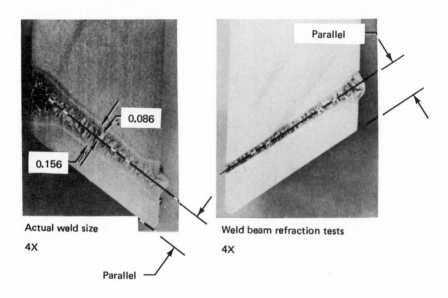

Fig. 10 – Weld beam refraction test results

With reference to beam alignment with the joint, the EBW machine operator was using correct procedures to align the beam. However, after alignment, the operator made a full power tack weld of very short duration on the weld joint to verify beam location. What he observed was a tack weld that appeared to have its center below the joint. He then proceeded to take what he believed to be corrective action, by moving the EB gun vertically up, until the tack appeared to be centered. Cross sections of these tack welds revealed that moving the tack weld to where it appeared to be centered caused incomplete fusion in the joints and subsequent weld quality rejection. What was overlooked by the operator was the very low surface tension of molten titanium and the effects of gravity. These two effects combined to cause sag in the surface of the tack weld, resulting in what appeared to be misalignment.

Immediately after correcting the incomplete fusion problem, another type of defect was encountered. Weld shrinkage defects appeared in the center of the weld at the weld run-on end of the rib. Weld run-on and run-off blocks then were added to the ribs, extending the amount of material to be trimmed from each end. It was soon determined that these blocks were effective only when the blocks were in contact with the entire area at the end of the rib. However, a little preheat in the area, in combination with the run-on block, consistently corrected the lack of fusion problem.

The electron beam alignment block and the weld run-on/run-off blocks are now machined as a single unit (see Fig. 11). Preheat is applied to each end by EBW from a point approximately three inches from each end of the rib out onto the run-on and run-off blocks. The full length of the rib joint then is EB welded by starting at either end of the run-on block and stopping on the run-off block at the other end of the rib. No smoothing or cosmetic weld passes are made.

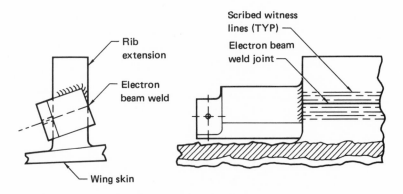

Fig. 11 — Beam alignment and weld run-on/run-off blocks

After welding, the previously scribed witness lines are used for visual inspection of the weld bead location. Then, radiographic and ultrasonic inspections are performed to verify weld quality after smoothing machine cuts are made on the front and back faces of the rib. A finished machined and formed Ti-6Al-4V lower inboard aft wing skin is shown in Fig. 12.

Fig. 12 – Lower inboard aft wing skin

Development of a Blind Tracking Device for Electron Beam Welding

The objective of this effort was to design, build, and test a "blind tracking device," (Fig. 13) which would automatically keep an EB gun centered over a blind component, such as a corrugation lying beneath a skin in a corrugated panel or cone assembly. The design of this unit was initiated because of the off-axis condition sometimes produced in long corrugations that are brake-formed in large, thin panels. Also, weld shrinkage causes the corrugations to bow laterally. The amount of bow is unpredictable and the problem is most severe in long, large diameter assemblies. In one case, the bow approached 0.1 inch (more than 1/2 corrugation width), which caused the electron beam to burn holes through the skin. Lateral misalignment of the corrugation ends made it necessary for the operator to make a trial spot weld at each end, then splitting the difference for the best center position of the weld. This lateral misalignment resulted in a loss of weld quality and required 96 hours to perform a nominal 16-hour welding task.

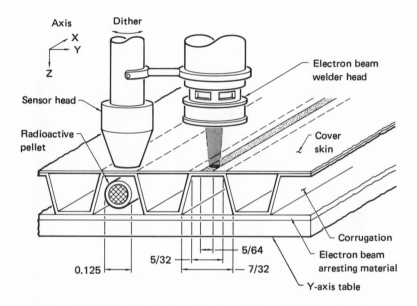

Fig. 13 – Cross section automatic blind tracking

Reducing the setup time also was a primary goal of the study. Successful completion of this effort would eliminate the need for a trial EB spot weld at each end of the corrugations to determine corrugation position with respect to EB gun travel, thus reducing setup time to a minimum.

Three, position detection systems were evaluated as possible solutions: (1) infrared, (2) radioactive pellets, and (3) magnetic. The most promising method used radioactive pellets and a sensing device (scintillation counter) coupled to electronic circuitry of the "blind tracking device" to control the EB welding machine servo-mechanism for automatic positioning. A study of the electrical system that controlled the servo-mechanism preceded formulation of the "blind tracking" electronic system. Commerical electronic components available inhouse were used including the radioactive pellet. The electronic components were assembled and mechanical components designed and fabricated. The system was bench tested, installed in the EB welding machine, and functionally tested (see Fig. 14).

Fig. 14 — Automatic blind tracker in EB weld chamber

The "blind tracking system" employs a low-intensity radioactive pellet encapsulated at the end of a flexible cable. In application, the pellet is fed into the corrugation adjacent to the corrugation to be welded and is driven by gears slaved to the EB gun. The pellet velocity is identical to the EB gun X-axis travel speed, thereby maintaining a position along this axis corresponding to the sensor head location. The sensor head, which is laterally displaced a corrugation width forward of the EB gun and above the radioactive pellet, is mechanically attached to the EB gun. Small lateral displacements between the sensor head and the pellet along the Y-axis due to bow in the corrugations are detected by oscillating the sensor head along the Y-axis and phase detecting the sensor output with respect to the oscillation (synchronous detection) via the signal processor. The error signal from the processor is used to energize the EB welding machine's Y-axis servo-mechanism, which positions the corrugations relative to the welding gun, thereby automatically maintaining the EB gun on the corrugation centerline.

Successful "blind tracking" was evidenced in test welds through a skin into a corrugation intentionally misaligned by as much as one-fourth inch in 18 inches. The test welds were not on a straight line. This was due to the lack of complete effectiveness of the pellet housing centering spring device. After improvement in the centering spring device, a frustum of a cone was EB welded (see Fig. 15).

Fig. 15 — EB welded skin to corrugations

This effort has resulted in the successful development of a new useful tool and capability at McDonnell Aircraft Company.

Diffusion Bonding in Superplastic Forming/Diffusion Bonding

John R. Williamson
Deputy Program Manager
Advanced Metallic Structures
Air Force Wright Aeronautical Laboratories

Introduction

Starting in the early 1960's and continuing through the 1970's, the Air Force funded a number of research and development programs in diffusion bonding of titanium. These programs involved the joining of titanium plate material in the general form of a desired final product. The purpose of these programs was to establish a process that would minimize the machining necessary to attain the final shape. In the mid '70's diffusion bonding was carried a step further when it was combined with another process, superplastic forming, to selectively thicken titanium sheet materials. Later efforts in conjunction with superplastic forming led to *selective diffusion bonding* of titanium sheet materials that were subsequently formed into complex shapes, such as honeycomb panels. This paper will discuss various studies conducted in combining diffusion bonding with superplastic forming and will provide examples of aircraft structures that have been fabricated, along with cost savings analyses.

The question always arises as to whether diffusion should be considered a bonding process or a welding process. Most people associate bonding with gluing, i.e., using a dissimilar material to hold the materials together. Though sometimes another material is used as a diffusion activator, diffusion bonding in its purest form does not involve the addition of dissimilar materials. On the other hand, most people associate welding as the joining of metals by heating to the melting point. In the diffusion bonding process, melting does not occur. To the contrary, too high a temperature can inhibit diffusion bonding. A broader definition of welding available from Webster's *New World Dictionary* is "to bring into close or intimate union; unite in a single, compact whole." It would be hard to find a definition that better fits diffusion bonding. Thus it is quite appropriate to consider diffusion bonding as a welding process. Most people, however, avoid the argument by classifying the process as a solid-state joining process.

Diffusion bonding for the purpose of this paper will be defined as a solid-state joining process, whereby pressure, temperature, and time result in the intimate union of two surfaces and the diffusion of these surfaces to form a single, compact material. Since this definition defines a process that is not typical of other welding processes, it is not surprising then that critical process variables result that are not typical of other welding processes. Considerable efforts have been conducted during the last five years to define these variables for performing diffusion bonding during the superplastic forming process.

The Process

During the development of the B-1, engineers at the Rockwell International Corporation discovered that Ti-6Al-4V exhibited superplasticity (the ability to resist necking during tensile elongation at high temperatures). It was found that titanium could be elongated over 1000 percent at temperatures of 1700 to 1750° F. Examination of this phenomenon led to the development of a superplastic forming process. This process depicted in Fig. 1A involves placing a sheet of titanium between two boxes (or tools). The titanium acts as a membrane. The box is placed in a constraining system, such as a hydraulic press, and then heated to 1650 to 1750° F. At this temperature gas is injected into one of the boxes, forcing the titanium membrane into the other box. The titanium then forms to the contour of the second box, which has been precontoured to some desired shape. When additional thickness of titanium is required, titanium details can be preplaced in the box. The sheet of titanium being formed into the box will diffusion bond to these titanium details. The pressures required to achieve this diffusion bonding are quite low. In diffusion bonding of plate materials, pressures of 2000 psi are typically used. These pressures are needed to move the mass of material to achieve intimate contact of the mating surfaces. In superplastic forming/diffusion bonding (SPF/DB) of sheet materials, however, such high pressures are not needed to achieve intimate contact. Typically pressures of 200 to 300 psi are enough to achieve the desired contact.

A second development was the selective diffusion bonding and forming application of the process. In this SPF/DB process depicted in Fig. 1B (Ref. 1), the titanium is selectively masked with a diffusion bonding inhibitor such as boron nitride (BN) or yttria (Y_2O_3). This maskant is applied to match a die cavity shape. Diffusion bonding is performed first by injecting gas into the lower tool (box) and forcing the two sheets of titanium together. After diffusion bonding has been achieved, the gas is evacuated and gas is injected through small tubes between the two sheets of titanium. The areas not diffusion bonded are then blown apart, forcing the lower sheet into the lower die cavity and resulting in an integrally stiffened structure.

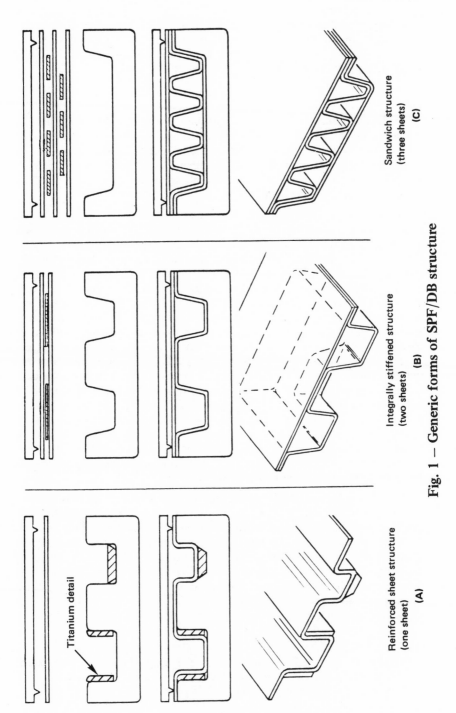

Titanium detail

Reinforced sheet structure
(one sheet)
(A)

Integrally stiffened structure
(two sheets)
(B)

Sandwich structure
(three sheets)
(C)

Fig. 1 – Generic forms of SPF/DB structure

The third development is a modification of the second application of the process. In this application three or more sheets are selectively masked, diffusion bonded together, then blown apart. This is shown in Fig. 1C (Ref. 1). By this approach, sandwich structures can be produced.[1]

Diffusion Bonding

There has been considerable discussion as to what diffusion bonding is and how it occurs. Much of this discussion centers around surface contact and grain growth. Some people argue that intimate contact results in a diffusion bond and that grain growth is not required. Arguments such as this will continue, since the basic metallurgical phenomenon "metallic bond" is still not completely understood.

Studies conducted to date show that the process is a function of pressure, temperature, and time. Rockwell International has developed an analytical curve for 100 percent diffusion bonding as a function of time and pressure at the superplastic forming temperature of 1700° F (see Fig. 2) (Ref. 1). Test data of experimental studies plotted on the figure (discussed below under "surface roughness") generally confirm the relationship. That more than simple diffusion is involved is clear from looking at Fick's first law of diffusion: $dm = -D(c/x)/Adt$. This equation states that the amount of material (dm) that crosses the plane of diffusion is equal to a diffusion coefficient (D) times the concentration gradient (c/x) that exists at the plane divided by the planar surface area (A) times the increment of time (dt). As can be seen, the only apparent process variable is time. This says that any two surfaces held in contact will over some time period eventually result in diffusion. The key is "over some time period." The diffusion coefficient for metals has a temperature dependence. At room temperature, the two surfaces may take hundreds of years for diffusion to occur. As temperature is increased, this process is greatly speeded up. But nowhere in the equation is pressure a factor, yet experimental studies show it to be very important. Therefore, something other than pure diffusion is occurring.

Dr. Howard Hamilton (co-inventor of the "Method for Superplastic Forming of Metals with Concurrent Diffusion Bonding" - Patent #3,920,175) (Ref. 2) has characterized diffusion bonding as consisting of four distinct steps: (1) development of intimate physical contact along the bond plane, (2) formation of the metallic bond, (3) interdiffusion, and (4) recrystallization and/or grain growth across the interface. A discussion of "steps" is slightly misleading in that it tends to suggest separate sequential mechanisms, when in actuality they are probably all occurring simultaneously. Figure 2 shows diffusion bonding to be a direct function of pressure. Of the four

---

1. United States Patents 3,934,441; 3,920,175; and 3,927,817 have been issued to C.H. Hamilton et al. of the Rockwell International Corporation on the three basic processes depicted in Figs. 1A, 1B, and 1C.

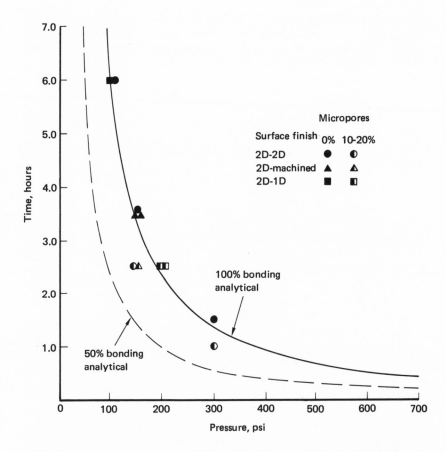

Fig. 2 – **Low-pressure diffusion bonding of Ti-6Al-4V sheet product at 1,700° F pressure vs minimum bonding time analytical curves compared to experimental results**

steps, only the first is primarily effected by pressure, i.e., pressure results in the materials creep forming together and deformation of surface irregularities, which provides the intimate contact. Since this figure only involves pressure and time, it tends to indicate then that these are the only important conditions and that achieving intimate contact is the only requisite. This is not true, but it is probably the rate controlling step in that the other steps occur much faster than the deformation processes (at least at low pressures). An analytical model for this time controlling phase has been developed by Dr. Hamilton and expanded upon by G. Garmong, N.E. Paton, and A.S. Argon (Ref. 3). One reason this step takes longer can be seen in a sketch of two surfaces at a point in the attainment of intimate contact:

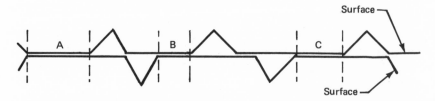

At points A, B, and C, intimate contact is already achieved and diffusion bonding is already occurring. So diffusion bonding incrementally occurs as the surfaces incrementally come into intimate contact. By the time the last surface areas come in contact (all voids are eliminated), it is likely that diffusion bonding (steps 2, 3, and 4 above) is complete. Garmong et al. conclude that the first step is dependent upon creep forming and diffusion of vacancies away from the bond region.

To suggest that intimate contact alone is sufficient can explain two metals being joined, but it cannot explain the strength of diffusion bond joints. Until atoms or molecules actually join, the only attractive forces existing between them are called Van der Waals forces. (Indeed this may be the primary mechanism occurring in adhesive bonding.) If these forces were in themselves adequate joining forces, the bond would be an atomic or molecular bond, but not a diffusion bond, by definition. Van der Waals forces, however, are secondary bond forces and "are weak in comparison with primary bonds (secondary bond strengths are of the order of magnitude of 1-5 kcal/mole; primary bond strengths are of the order of 20-50 kcal/mole)" (Ref. 4). Therefore, the primary bond is a more important contributor to the strength of the joint. This bond, normally referred to as a metallic bond, involves the sharing by atoms of each other's electrons. When atoms share electrons, they try to surround themselves by as many similar atoms as possible. This collection of atoms becomes a crystal or grain. If intimate contact alone resulted in a bond, it would mean that atoms at one surface have now joined atoms of the second surface to form a new grain. This would result in a joint as follows:

Original interface ⟶

First, the author has never seen such a boundary occur. Secondly, such a surface with nonrandomized grain boundaries would represent a weak joint. If, however, it is assumed that atoms of one surface have joined atoms at the second surface, then new grains have been formed across the surface. Such a randomization of grains would help to optimize the bond strength. To achieve a diffusion of atoms, it is necessary for some activation energy level to be achieved. This energy can come from four sources. Surface atoms have higher energies because they have unbalanced forces. (In liquids this is called surface tension.) These energies are not high enough by themselves to cause an atom to move from one grain to another. Temperature and pressure both add energy and contribute to the mobility. The fourth area is an energy imbalance between different sized grains. "...small grains have higher strain energies and are more unstable than larger grains. Therefore, if the temperature is increased in a solid, atoms diffuse across the boundaries from the smaller to the larger grains. The net result of this diffusion is the growth of the larger grains at the expense of the smaller ones, a phenomenon called grain growth." (Ref. 4).

The final point in this diffusion bonding discussion involves recrystallization. As indicated above, the most important step is achieving intimate contact. This involves plastic deformation of the material. Such plastic deformation results in strained, high energy regions. As the temperature is raised on such a material, the thermalization of atoms results in the formation of small, strain-free regions. These regions then grow in size and at the expense of their strained neighbors, again resulting in grain growth and reduction in strain (Ref. 4). An interesting point is that the plastic deformation is localized and can lead to grain growth at the bond line without grain growth in the material as a whole.

If the above did not confuse the issue enough, further discussion could also be provided on the importance of grain boundaries in the plastic deformation process and the role of vacancies, grain boundary dislocations, etc., on the diffusion of surface impurities and microvoids. However, the purpose of the above discussion is to point out the complexity of the process and to introduce the importance of the diffusion bonding variables to be discussed below.

Diffusion Bonding Variables

The primary factors effecting diffusion bonding are the *process variables,* i.e., pressure, temperature, and time, and the *material variables,* i.e., flow stress and strain, rate sensitivity of the material, surface roughness, surface cleanliness, and grain size. Two additional factors become important because of the nature of the process. When forming must occur prior to bonding (as in Fig. 1A), it is necessary to maintain the surfaces to be bonded in a noncontaminated, nonoxidized condition. Secondly, when a maskant is used for selective diffusion bonding (as in Figs. 1B and 1C), it is important to assure that the material used as a maskant does not interfere with diffusion bonding in the adjacent nonmasked areas. Much work has been done to understand the effects of all of the above variables. Some of the observations resulting from these studies will be presented.

Process Variables. It is difficult to discuss the variables of pressure, temperature, and time independently, since they are to some extent dependent variables. But by holding one of the variables as fixed, the dependency of the other two variables can be studied and thus the relative importance of each variable can be examined.

Pressure. Figure 2 as discussed above shows a direct relationship between time and pressure with diffusion bond strength. The analytical relationship was based upon the plane strain deformation theory and superplasticity involved in creep deformation. This would indicate that creep forming is the controlling factor and totally determines process time. However, the testing done to date has been limited, and it is possible that there might be process conditions that would result in other variables becoming the controlling factors. For example, the curve indicates that higher and higher pressures will result in shorter and shorter process times. However, it might be possible through very high pressure to achieve intimate contact so quickly that diffusion, grain growth, and metallic bonding have not completely occurred. In tests conducted by Grumman Aerospace (Ref. 5) (see Fig. 3), diffusion bonding was conducted at 1200 psi for one hour at 1700° F and parent metal strengths were not achieved. A primary difference in the data plotted in Fig. 2 and that plotted in Fig. 3 is the fact that one study was done based upon elimination of micropores and the other was based upon achieving parent metal strength. It will be seen later that elimination of micropores is not mandatory for parent metal strength. Therefore, pressure is important in getting the surface in intimate contact and for normal operation may be the controlling variable, but other variables such as surface, grain size, temperature, etc., can significantly affect the curve shown in Fig. 2.

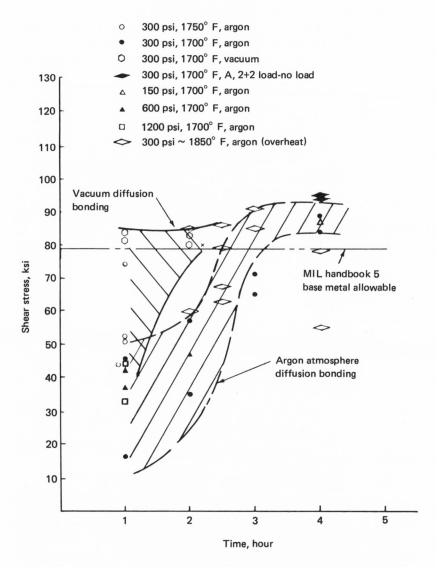

Fig. 3 – Effect of diffusion bonding time on lap shear strength

Temperature. Since the superplastic forming process is done typically in the 1650 to 1750° F range, the diffusion bonding studies have also been done in this range. This range is not broad enough to cause drastic differences in diffusion bonding. In general, the higher temperatures will give slightly shorter diffusion bond times or higher strengths for the same diffusion bonding time. Figure 3 shows that 1750° F gives higher strengths at one hour than 1700° F with the same process conditions. However, as parent metal strength is approached at 2-1/2 hours, the difference disappears. If temperatures get too high, the beta transus is reached. In the beta condition the material loses its superplasticity and rapid grain growth occurs. This is an interesting study for diffusion bonding. Beta transformed materials, in general, do not diffusion bond very well due to a lack of superplasticity (thus more difficult to achieve intimate contact) and because of the large grain sizes and less energy available for atom mobility. Yet when starting with normal material and then heating it to the beta transus temperature during the SPF/DB process, it is possible to get excellent diffusion bonds (see Fig. 3). In this case, apparently the material has time to creep form to intimate contact before the beta transus is reached and then the rapid grain growth actually assists in achieving diffusion. On the other hand, if the temperature gets too low, the superplasticity is less, and longer times are necessary to achieve intimate contact. Likewise, the diffusion rate is also slowed down and could also effect the time for complete bonding.

Time. Time is an important variable for several reasons. First, creep forming is time dependent, resulting in a minimum time (depending on pressure and temperature) to achieve intimate contact. Secondly, in a process such as shown in Fig. 1A, the titanium sheet must superplastically form to finally come in contact with the piece of titanium that is to be diffusion bonded. Depending on the titanium sheet thickness, this can require in the range of one hour. If the tooling must be heated from room temperature to the superplastic forming temperature also, it is possible that the titanium has been subjected to high temperatures for well over two hours. This creates two problems. It is extremely difficult to maintain an inert atmosphere in the tool. Because of this the titanium tends to develop an alpha case that can prevent diffusion bonding. Secondly, the grains will grow with temperature (discussed further below under grain size). The grain growth reduces energy available for atom mobility and also increases the flow stresses needed to achieve intimate contact.

Material Variables

Surface Roughness. There has not been an extensive evaluation of this area, since as-received surface finishes have not resulted in any significant diffusion bonding problems. Engineers at Rockwell International Corporation (Ref. 1) have examined three different surface finishes: a mill 2D finish (cold-rolled, sheet metal specification finish), a mill 1D finish (hot-rolled, descaled, and grit blasted, plate material specification finish), and a machined finish of 63 RHR (a good machined surface finish, typically required on fatigue critical aircraft parts). As indicated previously, Rockwell has established a theoretical minimum pressure-temperature curve for obtaining a 100 percent diffusion bond of Ti-6Al-4V sheet material. Utilizing three combinations of materials (sheet-to-sheet [2D to 2D], sheet-to-machined [2D to machined], and sheet-to-plate [2D to 1D]), Rockwell selected conditions on or just above the minimum curve and conditions under the minimum curve to produce test specimens. All sheet-to-sheet and sheet-to-machined plate specimens on or above the curve exhibited 100 percent bonding (see Fig. 2). Those conditions under the curve showed 10 to 20 percent porosity and gave validity to the curve. It was also seen that the rougher surface on the 1D plate material did not achieve a 100 percent bond for conditions above the minimum curve. As discussed above under "Process Variables," the first stage of diffusion bonding requires a creep forming of the material together to overcome surface irregularities. Apparently, the rougher surface lengthens the time necessary to achieve intimate contact and the analytical prediction needs to be adjusted when rougher surfaces are involved. It is anticipated that most of the diffusion bonding will be done with sheet material and machined inserts, and thus the analysis is reasonably accurate and no problems are anticipated.

Surface Cleanliness. Any surface contamination can affect diffusion bonding. Therefore, prior to bonding it is critically important to chemically clean and pickle all titanium blanks and details in accordance with MIL-S-5002 and MIL-C-81769 to provide surfaces free of grease, cutting fluids, markings, dirt, chips, chlorides, and alpha case. At high temperatures, titanium has often been called a universal solvent. But even if it were able to absorb all of the contaminates on an uncleaned surface, it would significantly affect processing conditions and could result in an inadequate bond.

The biggest problem to date has not been in obtaining clean enough surfaces for diffusion bonding. It has been in keeping the surfaces clean. As mentioned above, in a process such as shown in Fig. 1A, it is possible to get an alpha case on the titanium. Diffusion bonding as it occurs in this process is called secondary bonding, since the material must form to the titanium details before bonding can initiate. If the alpha case forms before contact, it can disrupt the diffusion bonding. In Fig. 1B, there is also a problem. The maskant material used to control the diffusion bonding pattern can "outgas," causing alpha case in the nonmasked areas. Fortunately, in this process the diffusion bonding is done before the forming, and the time available for contamination to occur is short.

One of the reasons it is difficult to maintain an inert atmosphere in the tool is that it is practically impossible to machine the upper and lower die surfaces to perfectly match. As the tools are heated, they will eventually creep together and seal, but it is possible for oxygen to get into the tool before a complete seal is obtained. Various techniques are used. Often a machined lip is used on one or both dies to press into the titanium sheets. Other techniques used to get a seal include the use of a metal wire that can be deformed between the tools; machined grooves, with argon flowed through the grooves; and the use of materials such as Grafoil. A different technique to avoid contamination is used by several other companies. In this technique, the two titanium sheets are welded together around their periphery. Prior to placing the titanium into the tool, the gas lines are attached to the welded pack and the pack is vacuum purged (1 x 10^{-2} torr or better) and backfilled with argon gas. This is typically repeated at least three times. After the last cycle, the pack is backfilled with argon to approximately atmospheric pressure and the pack is placed in the die.

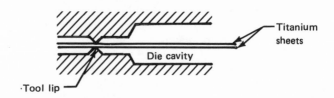

McDonnell Aircraft Company (Ref. 6) has conducted studies on the possibility of the maskant material causing alpha case in adjoining nonmasked areas. Figures 4 through 7 show some of the results. As can be seen (Fig. 4) when a lucite, butyl acetate, and acetone binder system was used, outgassing occurred, resulting in an alpha case in the nonmasked areas. If, however, a vacuum is pulled on the pack, it is possible to eliminate the volatile materials and thus reduce alpha case (Fig. 5). The other systems examined were boron nitride and yttria, both with Plastibond "B" as the binder (Figs. 6 and 7). Neither system caused significant alpha case in the nonmasked areas; however, boron nitride did result in alpha case on the surfaces it contacted (Fig. 7). The recommended system is yttria with a suitable organic binder such as Plastibond "B" or butyl acetate. This is important to recognize not only for parts produced by process shown in Fig. 1B or 1C, but also for parts produced as in 1A. This is because boron nitride and yttria are also used as lubricants sprayed on the die surface.

The importance of this area cannot be over-emphasized. The author is aware of numerous instances in which an alpha case has resulted during secondary bonding. When the parts were taken from the tooling, the bonds were so weak that they fell apart.

Grain Size. Grain size is an important variable in SPF/DB for a number of reasons. Most of these have been discussed above. Large grain size reduces superplasticity. In Fig. 1A type processing, this results in the forming sheet taking considerably longer to reach the bonding details and inadequate time available for the diffusion bonding can result. Figure 8 shows that to go from a 6.4 μm to a 11.5 μm grain size can result in a process forming time increase from 30 minutes to well over 150 minutes. The larger grains themselves result in longer diffusion bonding times (probably due to higher flow stresses and thus longer times required to creep form the surfaces to intimate contact and due

Location A - Contaminated bond area

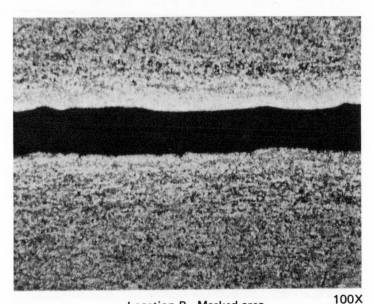

Location B - Masked area   100X

Fig. 4 – Photomicrographs of samples removed from panel 2-4 lucite, butyl acetate, acetone, and yttria with argon gas

Location A - Contaminated bond area

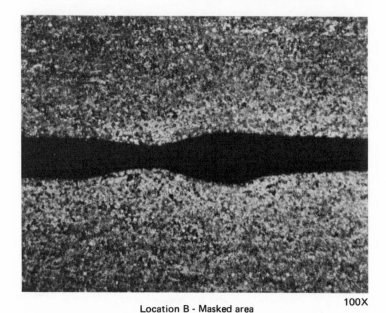

Location B - Masked area

100X

Fig. 5 — Photomicrographs of samples removed from panel 2-5
lucite, butyl acetate, acetone, and yttria with vacuum

Location A - Bonded area

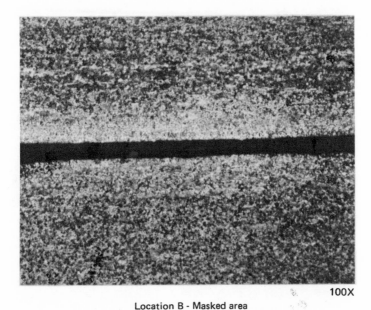

100X

Location B - Masked area

Fig. 6 — Photomicrographs of samples removed from panel 2-5B plastibond "B" + yttria with argon gas

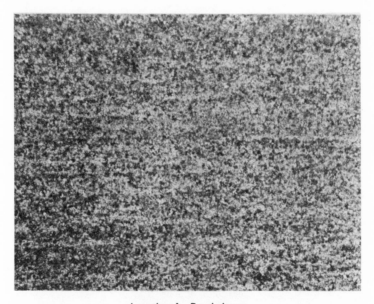

Location A - Bonded area

Location B - Masked area   100X

Fig. 7 — Photomicrographs of samples removed from panel 2-2 plastibond "B" + boron nitride with argon gas

SPF

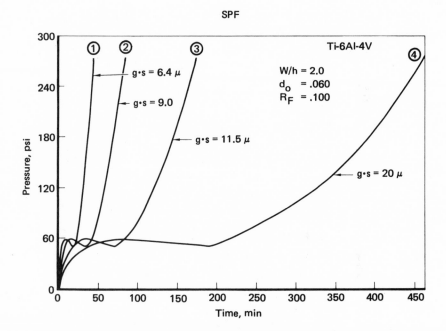

Fig. 8 — Effect of grain growth on SPF

DB

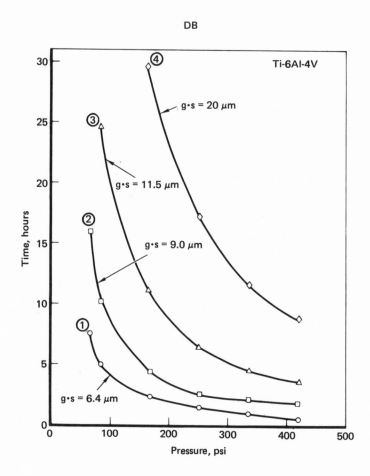

Fig. 9 – Effect of grain growth on DB

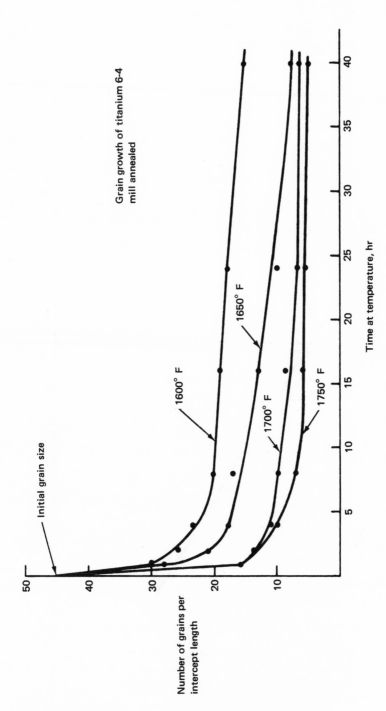

Fig. 10 — Effect of temperature and time on grain growth

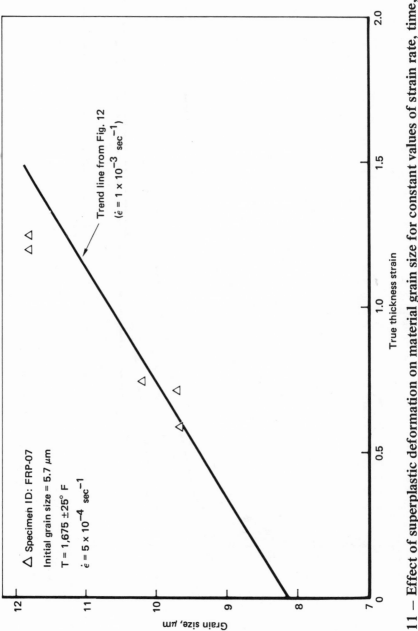

Fig. 11 — Effect of superplastic deformation on material grain size for constant values of strain rate, time, and temperature; $\dot{\epsilon} = 5 \times 10^{-4}$ sec^{-1}

to higher energy required to obtain diffusion). Figure 9 (Ref. 7) shows the effect of grain size on diffusion bonding. At a grain size of 6.4 μm, the diffusion bonding occurred in about two hours at 200 psi. Whereas, at a grain size of 11.5 μm, about eight hours were required. (Both of the preceeding facts become extremely important because of grain growth during the process, as discussed below.) Generally grain size under 10 μm has been required in the starting titanium material. Fortunately, the normal mill annealed sheet product has almost always met this requirement. (Beware, though, that if plate product is used as a bonding detail, it can have significantly higher grain size than the sheet material.)

Grain growth during processing is significant and can greatly affect processing conditions. Figure 10 (Ref. 5) shows the effect of time and temperature on grain growth. (Grumman uses the number of grain boundaries intercepted by a standard 143 μm line at 400X magnification.) Of significance, particularly in Fig. 1A type processing, is that most of the grain growth occurs in the first one or two hours. Additionally, grain growth occurs because of the strain that results during forming. As discussed above under "Diffusion Bonding," plastic deformation results in strained high energy regions. Atoms migrate from the strained regions to unstrained or energy-free regions resulting in grain growth. Figure 11 (Ref. 8) shows the effect of strain on grain growth (temperature and time were held constant to independently assess the effect of total strain). It might also be noted on the figure that the starting material had a grain size of 5.7 μm; therefore, the grain size at 0 strain (approximately 8.2 μm) is due strictly to temperature. Figure 12 (Ref. 8) shows this grain growth in a formed hat shape. If it had been desired to bond a strip on the top of the hat, the diffusion bond cycle would have been much longer because of the grain size.

Whether grain growth or recrystallization, or both, are necessary to achieve diffusion bonding has been discussed above. There is reportedly evidence that suggests diffusion bonds can be created without grain growth or recrystallization, or both. However, this is immaterial, in that the factors that probably are necessary (atomic diffusion, plastic deformation, etc.) all tend to result in grain growth. Recrystallization and grain growth can result in growth of grains across the original interface, helping randomize grain boundaries, further extend and strengthen atom-to-atom bonds, and cause further disruption of the surface films at the joint. Figures 13 and 14 (Ref. 5) show some relationships between grain size and shear strength. An almost linear relationship was achieved between grain size and shear strength. Extremely important are specimens DB12B and DB7A in Fig. 13. Both of these specimens exceeded the Mil Handbook 5 shear strength value for Ti-6Al-4V (79 ksi), and yet intimate contact had not been completely achieved, as evidenced by the voids that are visible.[2]

---

2. It should be noted in all of the above discussions that grain size has to be taken with some degree of caution, since grain size can be greatly affected by the cooling rate of the structure.

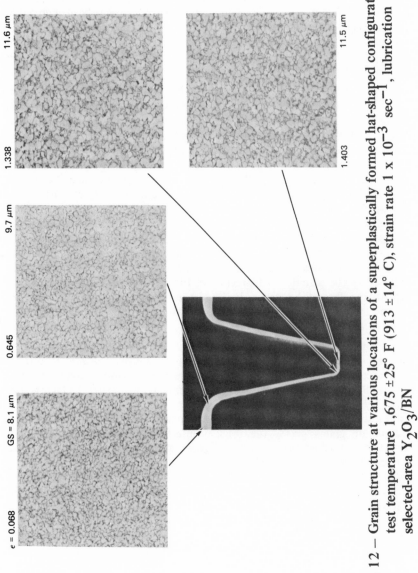

Fig. 12 — Grain structure at various locations of a superplastically formed hat-shaped configuration; test temperature 1,675 ±25° F (913 ±14° C), strain rate 1 x 10^{-3} sec^{-1}, lubrication selected-area Y$_2$O$_3$/BN

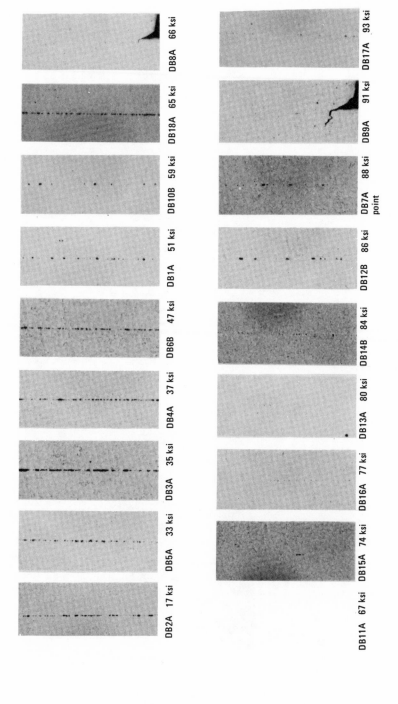

Fig. 13 — Photomicrographs of typical bond-line defects observed in section through doubler (200X mag)

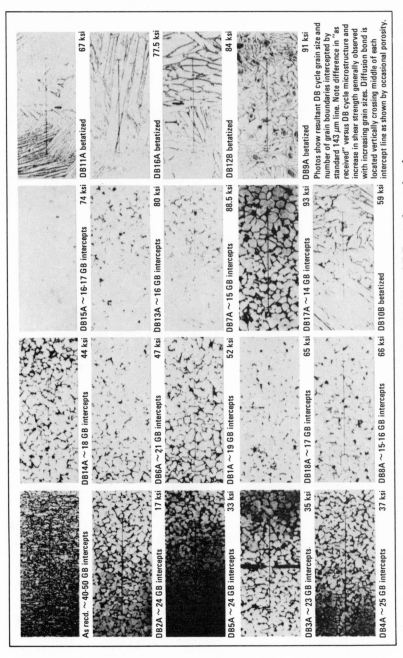

Fig. 14 — Photomicrographs (400X) of DB cycle grain size

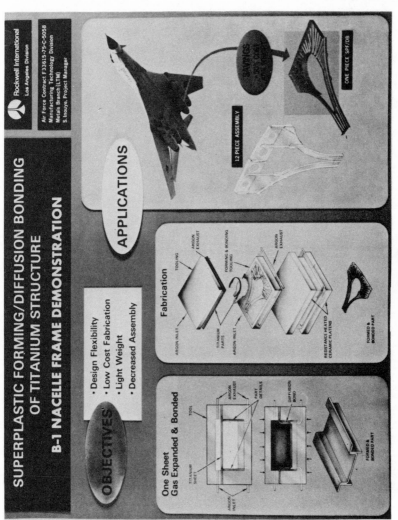

Fig. 15

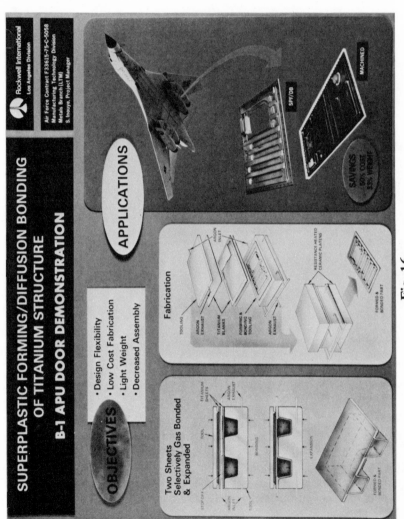

Fig. 16

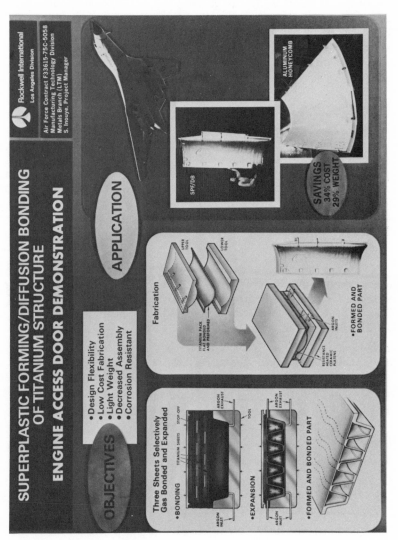

Fig. 17

Superplastic Forming/Diffusion Bonding Applications

Examples of components fabricated by processes depicted in Figs. 1A, 1B, and 1C are shown in Figs. 15, 16, and 17, respectively. Because of the ability to eliminate fabrication and assembly of numerous details and the ability to design more structurally efficient designs, cost and weight savings of 50 percent and 30 percent respectively have been achieved consistently. Because of these tremendous reductions and the flexibility of the process, it is expected that no future Air Force aircraft requiring titanium will be built without using this process.

Summary

The superplastic forming/diffusion bonding process has been a major materials breakthrough in the fabrication of titanium structures for aerospace applications. Much is still unknown about what is actually happening during the process. This paper has presented numerous observations and offered discussion as to what *can* be happening. The important point is that the process works and has demonstrated the potential for revolutionary savings in cost and weight of titanium aircraft structures. If there are to be future high speed aircraft such as a supersonic transport or Mach 3 aircraft, this technology will almost certainly play a major role.

References

1. E.D. Weisert; G.W. Stacher; and B.W. Kim. May 1979. *Manufacturing methods for superplastic forming/diffusion bonding process,* AFML-TR-79-4053, final report AF contract F33615-85-C-5058. Rockwell Internal, Los Angeles, California.

2. C.H. Hamilton. 1973. *Titanium science and technology.* Proceedings of the Second International Conference, R.I. Jaffee and H.M. Burte, eds., vol. 1, p. 625. New York: Plenum Press.

3. G. Garmong; N.E. Paton; and A.S. Argon. June 1975. Attainment of full interfacial contract during diffusion bonding. *Metallurgical Transactions* vol. 6A, pp. 1269-1279.

4. R.W. Hanks. 1970. *Materials engineering science - an introduction.* New York: Harcourt, Brace and World, Inc.

5. C. Paez. August 1979. *Built-up low-cost advanced titanium structures (BLATS),* AFFDL-TR-79-3093, final report AF contract F33615-77-C-3109. Grumman Aerospace Corporation, Bethpage, New York.

6. C.M. Fleming, and D.J. Chronister. May 1980. *Superplastic forming/ diffusion bonding (SPF/DB) process limits,* AFML-TR-80-4047, final report AF contract F33615-77-C-5208. McDonnell Douglas Corporation, St. Louis, Missouri.

7. S.P. Agrawal, and E.D. Weisert, Rockwell International Corporation. Private communication, 1980.

8. S.P. Agrawal, and E.D. Weisert. *Superplastic forming/diffusion bonding (SPF/DB) process capabilities and limits,* IR-780-7(111), interim report AF contract F33615-78-C-5016. Rockwell International Corporation, Los Angeles, California.

Aluminum and Its Alloys: Weldability

I.B. Robinson
Kaiser Aluminum and Chemical

Introduction

Aluminum alloys played an important part in the history of aviation and aerospace, even prior to the Wright brothers' engine cylinder block (Ref. 1). They continue to fill a major role as evidenced by the current work on the welded aluminum external tank and crew module for the Space Shuttle (Refs. 2 and 3).

A prime aerospace goal has always been to provide necessary structural strength at a minimum weight, thus the drive to achieve the maximum strength-to-weight ratio. From published property data you can pick an alloy and temper to provide highest mechanical properties, good fracture toughness, low fatigue crack growth rate, or best performance at cryogenic or elevated temperatures. Then someone must decide how the final structure will be fabricated.

The more complex a structure, the more parts that must be joined in some way to fabricate a completed, usable assembly. The ease of joining or the weldability of an alloy will vary widely with its composition and microstructure, and the alloy mechanical properties will also vary with composition and microstructure.

It turns out to be understandable, but still disappointing, that the highest strength alloys are often the most difficult to join, especially by fusion methods.

For this reason the strongest alloys have historically been joined by mechanical fasteners, rivets, and resistance spot welds for aircraft construction. The penalty in terms of overall weight and performance has been accepted in order to gain product reliability and allow fabrication with proven processes.

If a weld could be made with properties approximating base metal properties, it would be a desirable joining method. We will review the problems encountered during welding aluminum alloys, why they occur, and what the prospects are for improving properties.

Aluminum Alloys

The variety of available aluminum alloys (Ref. 4) can be divided into two major classes: non-heat-treatable (NHT) and heat-treatable (HT). In addition, they can be classified and compared by the major alloying constituents.

85

The tensile properties of selected NHT and HT alloys are shown in Fig. 1 for the annealed temper. This shows that strength depends on the amount and type of alloying additions made to pure aluminum. Annealed NHT alloys can have higher strengths than annealed HT alloys.

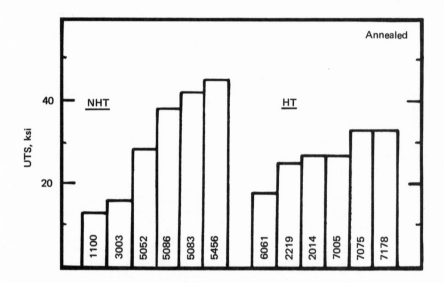

Fig. 1 — Strength comparison of selected, annealed aluminum alloys

When the tensile properties of the same alloys in their strain hardened (-HXX) or thermally treated (-TXX) tempers are compared (Fig. 2), the results change. The highest strengths are achieved by the HT alloys.

Newer alloys such as 2124, 7175, 7475, 7049, 7050, etc., are modifications or extensions of older established alloys. They often provide better fracture toughness, lower fatigue crack propagation, or improved resistance to stress-corrosion cracking or exfoliation corrosion. Their behavior in terms of fusion weldability is essentially the same as their predecessors, such as 2024 and 7075.

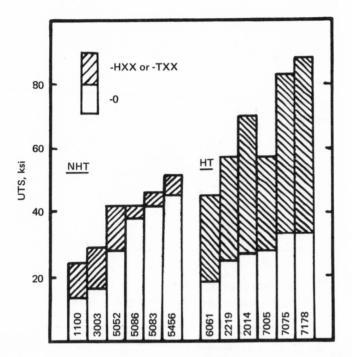

Fig. 2 — Strength comparison of selected aluminum alloys in strain hardened or thermally treated tempers

Metallurgical Behavior. The behavior of aluminum alloys during welding can be explained by the metallurgical reactions occurring during normal processing, but the times involved are much shorter.

Non-heat-treatable alloys gain strength from alloying additions and subsequent strain hardening (cold work) (see Fig. 3). In general, more cold work and greater alloying additions give higher strength and lower elongation (ductility).

When these alloys are exposed to reheating, they lose strength by recovery (up to 450° F), recrystallization (500 to 700° F) (Fig. 4) and grain boundary melting (1050° F and up). Annealed material is unaffected below the point of partial melting, but strain hardened material is reduced to -0 properties at annealing temperatures (see Fig. 5).

Although commercial treatments use times in terms of hours, the same reactions start in the seconds of high-temperature exposure seen during fusion welding. Regardless of the starting temper (strength) of a NHT alloy, there will be heat-affected zones that approach or, if times at temperature are sufficient, reach annealed properties (see Fig. 6).

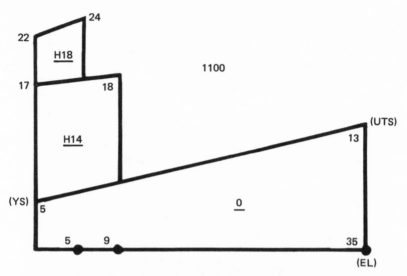

Fig. 3 — Tensile property comparison of commercially pure aluminum in annealed, half hard and full hard tempers

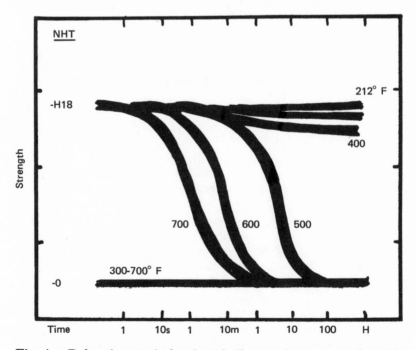

Fig. 4 — Reheating strain hardened alloys reduces strength, with time at temperature. Tested at room temperature.

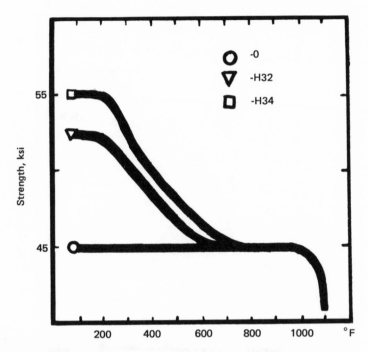

Fig. 5 — Alloy 5083 samples heated one-half hour at elevated
temperature, then tested at room temperature.
Regardless of starting condition, all tempers are
annealed around 650 to 750° F. Above 1000° F partial
(grain boundary) melting lowers annealed strength.

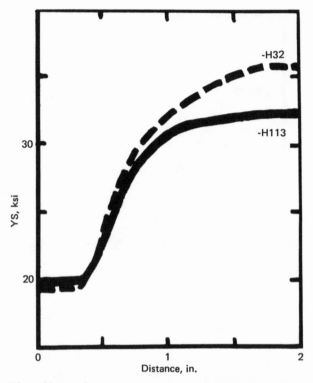

Fig. 6 — The effect of starting temper on yield strength properties of the HAZ in 5083 welds (Ref. 12)

Heat-treatable alloys gain strength by subjecting controlled alloying elements to planned thermal treatments. Three tempers are frequently encountered (see Fig. 7): the annealed (-0), the solution-treated and naturally aged (-T4), and the artifically aged (-T6). As with NHT alloys, higher strengths go with lower elongations. The systems must have relatively high solid solubility at elevated temperatures and low equilibrium solubility at room temperatures.

Solution heat treating will take the alloying constituents into solid solution (-W). They are retained by rapidly quenching the alloy. Natural aging can then occur at room temperature with time by the forming solute atom clusters to reach a stable -T4 temper (see Fig. 8).

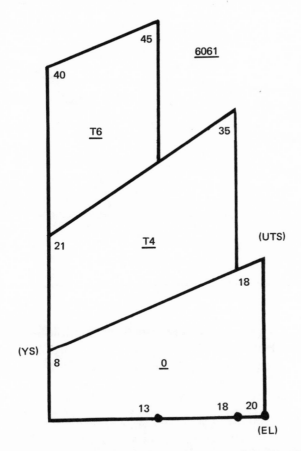

Fig. 7 — Tensile property comparison of heat-treatable alloy 6061 in the annealed, solution heat treated and naturally aged and artificially aged tempers

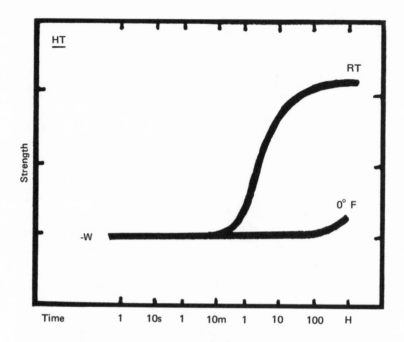

Fig. 8 — Time-temperature effects on solution treated alloy. Holding at 0° F retards natural aging. At room temperature natural aging develops the -T4 temper.

By using elevated temperatures, artificial aging, the strength can be greatly increased to form -T6 temper (see Fig. 9). The phenomenon of reversion is shown by the decrease in strength when the natural aging precipitate is taken back into solution before the artificial aging precipitate is formed. The aging precipitate atom clusters or G.P. zones provide strengthening up to a certain time. Continued aging or use of higher temperatures will lead to the formation of an equilibrium precipitate (overaging), continued particle growth, and annealing. Beyond a peak aging time-temperature, a loss in strength will occur. Some overaging can be desirable to improve other properties such as resistance to stress-corrosion.

Again, although minutes or hours are required for commercial processing (see Fig. 10), significant reactions and loss of properties can occur in seconds during welding (see Fig. 11). The figure shows that increased heat input increased both the width of the heat-affected zone (HAZ) and the amount of property reduction, by increasing time at temperature.

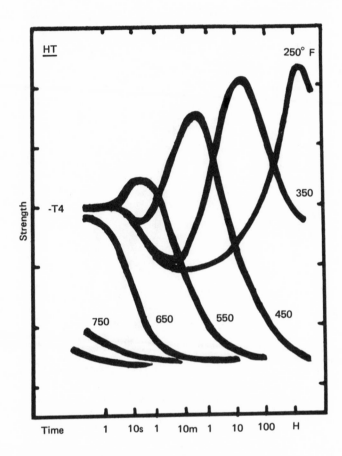

Fig. 9 — Isothermal heating of -T4 temper in the 200 to 500° F
range first causes reversion of the RT precipitate, then
artificial aging and overaging. Above 600° F
annealing occurs.

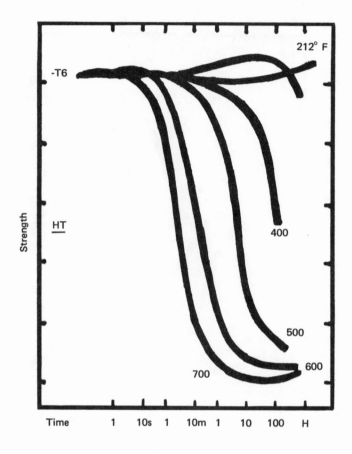

Fig. 10 – Reheating -T6 temper alloys causes overaging
and property loss.

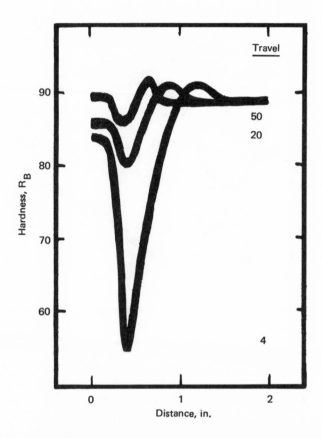

Fig. 11 — Varying heat input by changing travel speed affects the extent and amount of HAZ. Alloy 6061-T4, postweld aged to -T6 temper (Ref. 13).

In summary, the HAZ of welds in NHT alloys approaches an annealed condition regardless of starting temper. The width depends on the amount of heat input. The HT alloys are more sensitive to time at temperature. Increased heat input results in greater reductions in strengths and increased width of HAZ. If the welding process introduces more heat or if preheating is used, the HAZ damage will be more severe (see Fig. 12). On the other side, highly concentrated energy sources such as electron beams give much less HAZ (see Fig. 13).

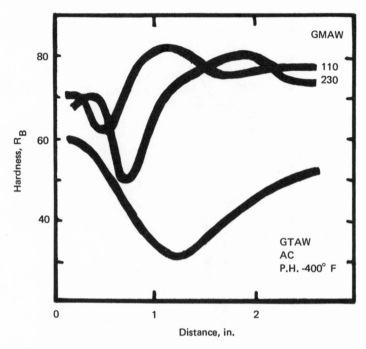

Fig. 12 — Increased heat input with GMAW and by GTAW
welding using a 400° F preheat widens the HAZ.
Alloy 2024-T4, 3/8-inch thick.

The HAZ properties in HT alloys depend upon alloy, starting temper,
and postweld treatment. Most of the HT alloys react similarly to 6061. As
shown in Fig. 14, as-welded -T6 material will have a minimum of around
700° F peak temperature and then higher properties around 900° F. The
overaged zone (700° F) does not respond well to postweld artificial aging,
while the solution-treated (900° F) zone will regain strength. Complete
postweld solution heat treating and aging will recover HAZ properties.

Welding on -T4 material produces a second dip around 400° F. This
indicates reversion of the natural aging precipitate. Postweld artificial aging
will recover most zones. The 700° F (overaging) region recovers better in -T4
material than in -T6 material, but not completely.

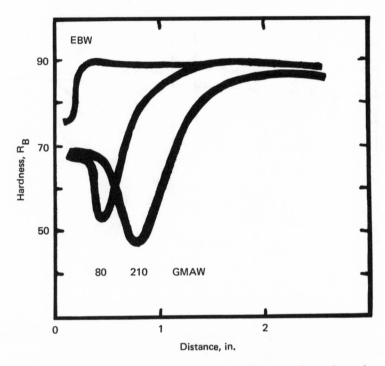

Fig. 13 — High energy sources such as EBW significantly reduce effective heat input and HAZ width compared to GMAW. Alloy 7075-T6, 1/2-inch thick.

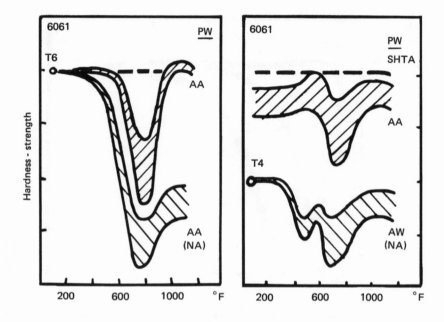

Fig. 14 – Representation of property changes at peak temperature locations in an alloy 6061 weld HAZ as affected by starting temper and postweld treatments

The weldable Al-Zn-Mg alloys (essentially those without Cu additions) respond much more readily to natural aging than do other HT alloys. Thus they can provide higher strengths after welding with only a period of natural aging rather than elevated temperature artificial aging. The general effects of starting with -T6 and -T4 tempers on the HAZ are illustrated in Fig. 15. Reversion of natural aging precipitate and recovery by natural aging are more pronounced. With these alloys the maximum loss in properties is near peak temperatures of 500° F. Again at 900° F and above solution takes place.

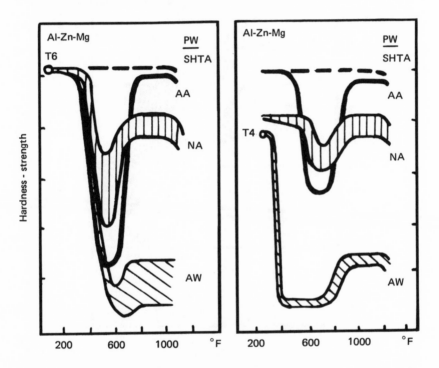

Fig. 15 — The effect of weld HAZ peak temperature on properties in weldable Al-Zn-Mg alloys. This is influenced by starting temper and postweld treatment.

Weldability of Aluminum Alloys. Basically, the greater the effective heat input used in making a weld, the lower the resulting mechanical properties. A reasonably good correlation can be obtained between heat input (kilojoules of weld heat per inch of weld per inch of material thickness) for the hottest weld pass and the resulting weldment tensile properties. This holds for both NHT and HT alloys (see Fig. 16). The rate of property decrease may well reflect one measure of weldability. Highest properties resulted from EBW, the lowest from using excessive heat.

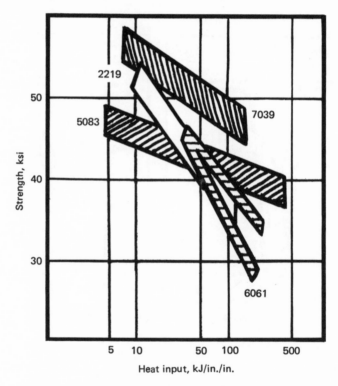

Fig. 16 — There is a general correlation between the effective heat input on a log scale and the resulting weld strength (6061 data from Ref. 13 and 2219 data from Ref. 14).

The overall effects of weld heat input reflect several factors. An increase in effective heat input can:

(1)   Decrease solidification rate of the weld, resulting in greater dendrite cell size and a decrease in mechanical properties (see Fig. 17).

(2)   Cause more melting and a wider weld bead. A decrease in width-to-thickness ratio will tend to higher properties.

(3)   Provide longer time at temper for metallurgical reactions.

Another measure of weldability is the combination of mechanical properties achieved.

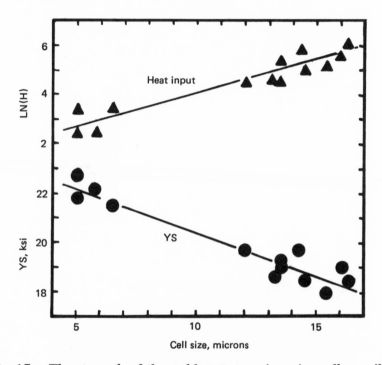

Fig. 17 – The strength of the weld cast zone, in a given alloy, will decrease with increased heat input (log scale). Heat input establishes solidification rate which controls dendrite cell size and resulting cast strength. Data for 5083/5183 welds.

Typical properties resulting from welding can be shown by means of simplified stress-strain representation diagrams (Ref. 5) (see Fig. 18). This shows UTS, YS, elongation, and a measure of toughness by the area encompassed. The weld properties are easily compared with the base metal.

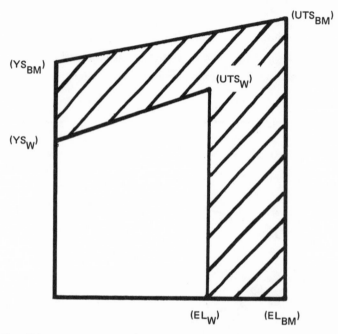

Fig. 18 — Diagram to provide visual comparison of weld (W) and base metal (BM) tensile properties (Ref. 5)

In a weldable HT alloy such as 5083, the parent metal properties can be approached by GMAW and GTAW procedures. EBW gives even higher properties. The use of solid-state welding (SSW) procedures (e.g., pressure welding and friction [inertia] welding) also produced welds approaching the base metal properties (see Fig. 19).

Alloy 6061 (Al-Mg-Si) is widely used but is not quite as weldable as NHT alloys when the resulting weld efficiency is considered. As shown in Fig. 20, postweld heat treatment by artifical aging (AA) or solution heat treating and aging (SHTA) can improve properties over as-welded levels. The more efficient results from solid-state welds is also seen.

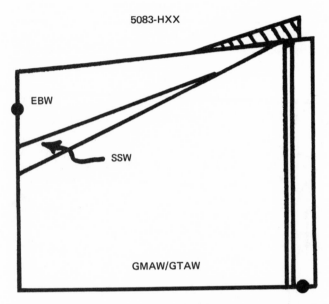

Fig. 19 — Welds, both fusion and solid-state, can approach the tensile properties of strain hardened 5083.

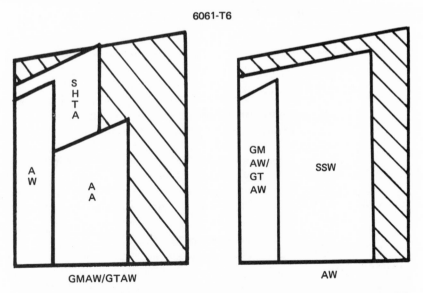

Fig. 20 — Fusion welds in 6061-T6 can be improved by postweld heat treatment. Solid-state welds have higher properties than fusion welds.

The weldable alloy 2219 (Al-Cu) is shown in Fig. 21. For GMAW and GTAW weldments, the best results are obtained by complete postweld solution heat treatment and aging. Postweld artificial aging reduced elongation, as typically occurs in HT alloys. The use of EBW significantly improved weld efficiency.

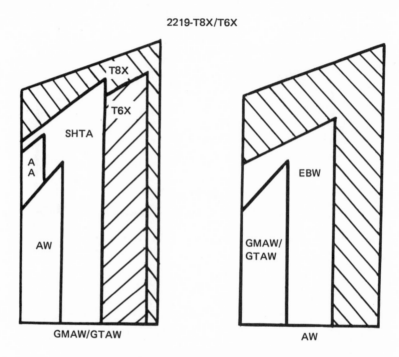

2219-T8X/T6X

Fig. 21 — Alloy 2219 welds respond well to postweld heat treatment and EB welds give significantly higher properties than GMAW/GTAW welds.

A less weldable 2000 series alloy 2014 (Al-Zn-Mg-Cu) is shown in Fig. 22. It shows greater difficulty in regaining weldment elongation than did 2219 alloy. The solid-state welds again performed better than fusion welds. High quality, mechanized welding and proper applications of weld properties have allowed the commercial use of fusion welded 2014.

The weldable 7000 series alloys (Al-Zn-Mg) can provide good weld efficiency with GMAW and GTAW procedures (see Fig. 23). Solid-state welds and EBW show good properties. There have been data showing that natural aging will continue for extended time periods and can reduce the toughness of weldments.

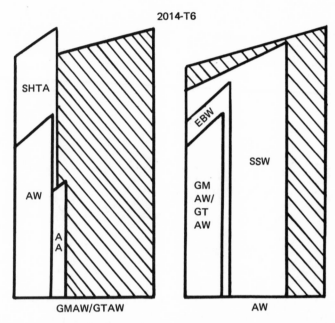

Fig. 22 — Alloy 2014-T6 is less weldable than 2219. Ductility
(elongation) may not be improved by postweld
treatments or EBW.

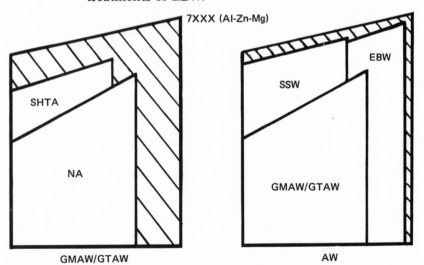

Fig. 23 — The weldable 7000 series alloys gain strength by
postweld natural aging and respond well to most
welding methods.

The more familiar 7000 series alloys such as 7075 (Al-Zn-Mg-Cu) are not usually considered as weldable. Figure 24 shows that regardless of postweld treatment, the elongation (ductility) of fusion welds remains low. In the as-welded condition, both EB welds and solid-state welds also give low ductilities. When welds are postweld solution heat treated and aged, only the solid-state welds markedly improved.

7075-T6

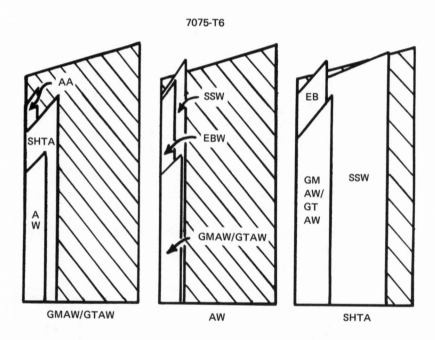

Fig. 24 — Alloy 7075-T6 welds show very low elongations. Only postweld solution heat treated and aged, solid-state welds approached parent metal properties.

Properties such as described above result in comparative performance (weldability) as reported in Ref. 6 (see Fig. 25). An initially lower strength alloy (2219) can provide higher weld properties than 2014 or 7075 in the presence of more severe welding conditions. From a property basis, it is more weldable.

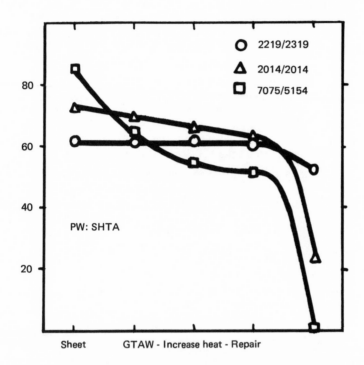

Fig. 25 — The effect of increased heat input and weld
discontinuities on strength can demonstrate
overall weldability of alloys (Ref. 6).

Summary

With existing alloys we can improve fusion welded joint properties by minimizing the effective heat input. This can increase weld solidification rates and improve properties. High intensity welding sources can provide greater penetration and narrower welds for higher strengths. Postweld heat treatments can improve properties. Poor fusion weldability of many high-strength alloys is dependent upon their composition and microstructure, and great improvements in fusion weldability and strength would require new alloys. Significant progress has been made in fusion welding heat-treatable aluminum alloys, particularly from work on missile, satellite, and space hardware (Refs. 2, 3, and 9). Continued work should provide additional advances (Refs. 7 and 10). Progress is expected in electron beam, laser beam, and plasma arc welding.

The current work on high quality, high-strength castings (Ref. 11) holds the potential and some promise for developing high efficiency welding of castings.

Solid-state welds minimize the problems of heat damage. These procedures coupled with heat treatment offer possibilities of higher strength welds in high-strength alloys. To some extent, processes that use both fusion and pressure (forging), such as resistance spot welding and flash welding in butt joints, may be usable for some joint configurations.

Material advances such as composites, fiber reinforcement, laminates, honeycomb panels, powder metallurgy products, and dispersion hardening have usually intensified the joining problems. Many of the improved materials (particularly combination materials) will probably not be suitable for fusion joining, but will rely on solid-state welding, adhesive bonding, mechanical fastening, and combinations thereof (Ref. 7).

Advances have been made in the use of structural adhesive bonding and combined processes such as weldbonding for aircraft (Ref. 8). Continued improvements can be expected in these areas, and their use should expand.

References

1. Burton, C.L. et al. Aircraft and aerospace applications. *Aluminum* Chapter 18, vol II. ASM.

2. Clover, F.R. 1980. Welding of the external tank of the space shuttle. *Welding Journal* 59(8): 17.

3. Whiffen, E.L. et al. 1980. Welding of the space shuttle orbiter crew module. *Welding Journal* 59(9): 17.

4. The Aluminum Association. Aluminum standards and data booklet.

5. Angermayer, K. 1966. Selection of structural aluminum alloys based upon welded properties. Aluminum Welding Seminar, Session 2, Paper 2, AA-AWS.

6. Collins, F.R. et al. 1961. Aluminum 2219: new alloy for high strength welded structures. *Metal Progress* 99(6): 82.

7. Mayfield, J.; Smith, B.A. et al. 1980. Joining technology for the 1980's. *Aviation Week and Space Technology* Feb. 8, 1980, p. 38.

8. Chandler, H.E. 1980. Challenges in aerospace materials and processes during the 80's. *Metal Progress* 118(2): 41.

9. Torgerson, R.T. and Christian, J.L. 1978. Materials and processes for the Tomahawk cruise missile. *Metal Progress* 116(2): 52.

10. Baxter, D.F. 1980. Survey report: welding in the 80's. *Metal Progress* 118(2): 28.

11. Goehler, D.D. 1978. Structural castings for aircraft: a progress report from Boeing. *Metal Progress* 116(2): 38.

12. Cook, L.A. et al. Properties of welds in Al-Mg-Mn alloys 5083 and 5086. *Welding Journal* 34(2): p. 112.

13. Burch, W.L. 1958. The effects of speed on strength of 6061-T4 aluminum joints. *Welding Journal* 37(8): 361s.

14. Parks, P.G. and Hoppes, R.V. 1966. Welding in aerospace applications. Aluminum Welding Seminar, Session 1, Paper 3, AA-AWS.

Keyhole Plasma Arc Welding of Aluminum

B.P. VanCleave and W.R. Gain
Boeing Aerospace Company

Introduction

By the 1960's, it had been well established that plasma arc welding in the keyhole mode offered some significant advantages over processes such as GMAW and GTAW for certain joint thicknesses in some materials. These advantages were significantly improved weld quality and decreased distortion, usually accompanied by a reduction in the number of weld passes.

Attempts to use the technique on aluminum were usually spectacularly unsuccessful. Use of DC power sources, in either straight or reverse polarity, exhibited severe cutting through the joint and complete lack of any fusion. AC power sources required high amperages to produce the keyhole, and then electrode deterioration became significant with a lack of weld pool control due to harmonic pulsing of the plasma gas column. Standard power sources would not provide the normal action of molten metal flowing smoothly around the keyhole and solidifying behind the arc as it traveled along the joint.

Exploratory tests were conducted using power sources with the capability of generating square wave reversing polarities with independent control of the positive and negative cycle times. The maximum cyclic ratios of straight-to-reverse times (in milliseconds) varied from 10:1 to 29:1.

These exploratory tests produced some welds and proved the feasibility of establishing a production process if a power source were available with wider ranges of independent control of straight and reverse polarity amperages and times.

Using available welding power supplies it was established that:

(1) Single polarity welding would not produce plasma arc welds in aluminum in the keyhole mode.

(2) AC welding would not produce enough heat at the work without generating too much heat at the electrode.

(3) Some reverse polarity would be required for cathodic cleaning the work surface of oxides.

(4) Alternating straight and reverse polarities would be required with the time (milliseconds) ratio somewhere in the range of 10:1 to 30:1.

(5) Independent control of straight and reverse polarity amperages would probably allow weld settings, providing appropriate heat and cathodic cleaning relationships.

Subsequent literature releases, in general, confirmed these findings: AC power sources could not be used for keyhole plasma arc welding of aluminum (Ref. 1); reverse polarity generated too much heat unless the workpieces were very thin (Ref. 2); reverse polarity cleaned the aluminum of oxides by cathodic sputtering (Refs. 2 and 3); and rectangular-shaped welding current wave forms provided more cathodic cleaning than sine wave forms (Ref. 3).

Schematically, the desired current, polarity and time relationships are shown in Fig. 1.

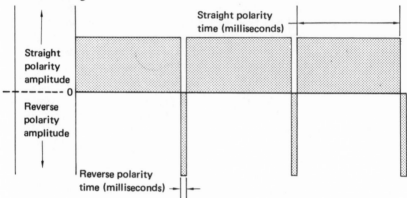

Fig. 1 — Conceptual current amplitude and time relationships

Development Procedure

A power supply was obtained that met the basic criteria established from the exploratory tests. The controller provided independently controllable current reversal times from 2.0 milliseconds to 999.0 milliseconds.

As shown in Fig. 2, oscilloscope traces of the current show, basically, a square wave form with different times and amplitudes for straight and reverse polarities.

The preliminary welding variables development was bead-on-plate work in the flat position followed by welding of square butt joints for final variable adjustments. This was done on 1/4 inch (6.3 mm) thick 2219-T87 aluminum plate until quality welds were consistently reproduced.

The preliminary welding variables development required trial and error changes in variables until the proper combinations were obtained to produce welds without "melt-thru" or "drop-thru." The variables considered are listed in Table 1 along with a general consideration given to weld quality, tungsten and orifice deterioration, and double arcing tendencies.

From the baseline welding variables for 1/4-inch (6.3 mm) thick 2219-T87 aluminum plate established in 1974, variables were established for various thicknesses of 2219 and for various thicknesses of additional aluminum alloys: i.e., 5456-H116, 5086-H32, 6061-T6, and A-356.

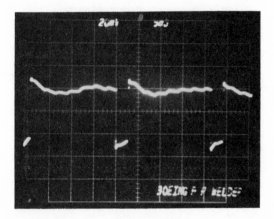

Fig. 2 — Oscillographic trace of "square wave" straight and
reverse polarity currents

Table 1
Preliminary welding variables development

Weld travel speed	Preweld cleaning technique
Orifice diameter	Straight and reverse polarity current amplitudes
Orifice gas pressure	
Shielding and backup gases	Straight and reverse polarity times
Filler wire speed and size	

Weld Characteristics

The developed weld procedures consistently produced keyhole welds typically shown in the Fig. 3 cross section macrograph.

Without filler wire addition, the limit of a single-pass keyhole weld, in the flat position, was 5/16 inch (8 mm). Thicker sections were welded; however, deviations from the square butt configurations were required, plus the addition of fill passes.

The square butt joint configuration shown in Fig. 4 resulted in consistent welds typically shown in the cross section macrograph. X-ray analysis on thousands of feet of welds show defect rates varying from zero to 0.5 percent (less than 1/2 inch defect in 100 inches of weld). Normally there was no defect identified by visual or penetrant inspection of these welds.

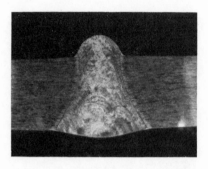

Fig. 3 — Cross section of aluminum keyhole weld (2.5X)

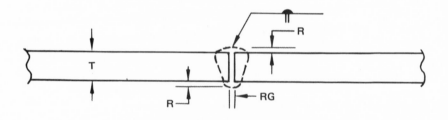

		Tolerance
● Thickness T	6.3 mm (0.25 in.) nominal	5.8 mm (0.23 in.) to 6.9 mm (0.27 in.)
● Mismatch		2.1 mm (0.08 in.) max
● Reinforcement (R)		1/3 T maximum
● Root gap (RG)		1 mm (0.04 in.) max

Fig. 4 — Typical square butt tolerances

Gross defects did occur when welding procedures were not followed or the root gap and mismatch were not within the tolerances shown in Fig. 4. Lack of adherence to welding procedures resulted in a complete lack of fusion as evidenced by "melt-thru." Normal care by skilled welders in following weld procedures avoided gross defects unless equipment malfunctions occurred. Equipment malfunctions were usually found to be in the torch and were attributed to improper maintenance and assembly or out-of-tolerance components.

Development Findings

Tungsten deterioration increased as the percentage (time and/or amplitude) of the reverse polarity cycle increased. A modified tip grind (more blunt) was required above 200 amperes. With only 3 milliseconds of reverse polarity current, the higher levels of heating were absorbed and electron impact damage was minimized.

Orifice life was not noticeably affected by the reversals of current flow. Double arcing did occur more readily than in conventional plasma welding because of the random change of location of current flow from the weld pool to the electrode in the reverse polarity portion of the weld cycle. Adequate orifice gas flow (pressure) was necessary to maintain the ionized conductor for the instantaneous reversal of weld current commensurate with maintaining optimum orifice gas velocities necessary for keyhole welding.

Orifice gas pressure pulsing was experienced and sometimes resulted in the expulsion of the weld pool through the keyhole. Orifice gas pressure pulsing could not be eliminated but was minimized without affecting the ionic (reverse polarity) cleaning process by adjustment of the straight to reverse polarity time ratio and corresponding number of polarity changes per second.

Shielding gas requirements beyond the standard torch-supplied flow were not required. The ability of the variable polarity current flow to continuously break down the oxide film and promote weld pool wetting precluded the requirement for secondary gas shielding.

Backup gas shielding was not required above the normal quantity of orifice gas projected through the keyhole during welding. The gas projection, in conjunction with the continuous arc cleaning process, provided adequate weld protection.

Filler wire additions into the weld pool did not require special equipment or techniques. Wire additions could be made into the keyhole when welding on materials of less than maximum thickness. A cosmetic wire pass was required when welding on materials approaching, or at, the maximum thickness of single-pass keyhole welds.

Cleaning

Reverse polarity cleaning action on the aluminum workpieces was evident as strips of bright metal (etched appearance) along the toe of the weld bead (see Fig. 5). This confirmed the original hypothesis concerning the cleaning action during welding and evidently was the primary force in obtaining keyhole welds: The molten metal flows onto and adheres to the oxide-free parent metal behind the keyhole. The surface tension of the molten weld metal and its adherence, apparently, were the major physical characteristics allowing plasma arc welding of aluminum in the keyhole mode.

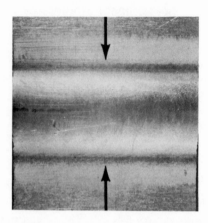

Fig. 5 – Cathodic cleaned areas adjacent to weld bead (1.75X)

Subsequent, but undocumented, tests indicated that any inclusions in the parent metal tended to float to the surface of the weld metal or were ejected through the keyhole to produce welds of a quality better than the parent metal. This was particularly noticed in forging and cast materials.

Welding Variables

A welding procedure for 1/4-inch (6.3 mm) thick 2219 is given in Table 2. Typical welding variables for various thicknesses of 2219 aluminum are shown in Fig. 6.

Travel speed and orifice pressure were straight-line functions of parent metal thickness. The straight and reverse polarity amperages were "S" type functions of thickness and had no simple relationship to each other.

Torch standoff distances are presented in Fig. 7 for various thicknesses of different alloys.

The straight and reverse polarity amperage relationships for various aluminum alloys in 1/4-inch (6.3 mm) thicknesses are given in Fig. 8. Detailed charts or tables identifying the welding procedures for various thicknesses of different alloys would be voluminous; however, the data given in Figs. 4, 6, 7, and 8 and Table 2 may be extrapolated to obtain approximate welding variables.

Table 2
Welding procedure for 2219 aluminum

Material	2219-T87	Orifice gas	Argon
Thickness	1/4 in. nominal (0.23 in. to 0.28 in.)	Orifice flow	8.5 ft^3/h
		Orifice gas pressure	1.3 lb/in.^{2}g
Weld position	Flat	Shielding gas	Argon
Power supply	300A variable polarity	Shielding gas flow	35 ft^3/h
Torch type	MPW–400A machine torch	Torch lag angle	5 deg
Weld current	140A straight polarity ±10%	Filler metal type	2319
		Filler metal diameter	1/16 in.
	180A reverse polarity ±10%	Filler metal speed	20 in./min ±10%
Current time	22 ms straight polarity 2 ms reverse polarity	Filler metal entrance angle	20 deg
Travel speed	7 in./min ±10%	Backup gas	None
Orifice diameter	0.125 in. ±0.002 in.	Trailer gas	None
Tungsten configuration	1/8 in. diameter 60 deg taper Round tip 0.325-in. extension	Torch standoff	1/4-in. (typical) ±10%

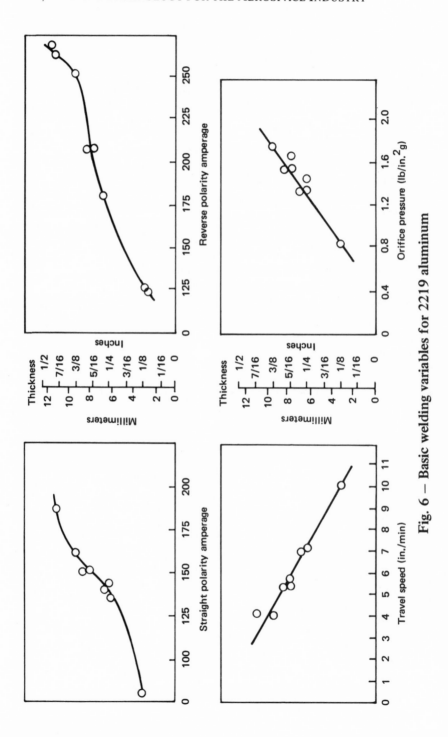

Fig. 6 — Basic welding variables for 2219 aluminum

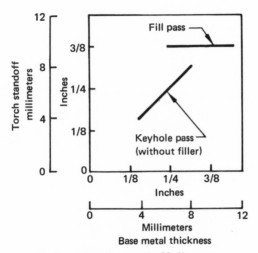

Fig. 7 – Torch standoff distances

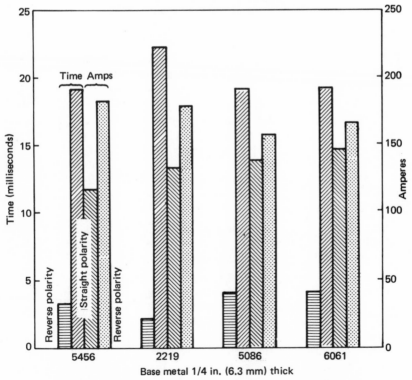

Fig. 8 – Current amplitude and time relationships for
aluminum alloys

The reverse polarity cleaning cycle removed oxides during welding, and the shielding gases prevented their reformation to provide surfaces that were wet by the molten weld metal; however, all oils had to be removed from the work prior to welding. Originally, the best method to ensure oil removal was vapor degreasing, alkaline cleaning, rinsing, handling with clean gloves, and then welding as soon as possible after cleaning. It was found that thorough vapor degreasing with subsequent contamination avoidance was adequate.

Welding of aluminum soon after cleaning has always been good practice, but with plasma arc welding there was added incentive: A minimum time lapse also meant less opportunity for inadvertent contamination with oils from any source. Generally, 24 hours was considered the maximum delay between vapor degreasing and welding. When longer delay periods were unavoidable, the joints were manually wiped with solvent immediately prior to welding.

Human oils, usually from fingerprints, were the main source of contamination; therefore, weld components had to be handled with clean, white gloves.

At first, hand filing of the prepared edges was used prior to welding the thicker materials. Filing was no longer required when careful machining, cleaning, and handling were observed to avoid burrs or nicks on the prepared edges.

Key Variable. The most important variable in keyhole plasma arc welding of aluminum was the ratio of straight-to-reverse polarity time. Welding could be accomplished only when the millisecond ratio of straight-to-reverse polarity current flow was approximately 20:3. The data are presented in Fig. 8.

The straight-to-reverse polarity current flow time ratio can be expressed in different ways: 80 percent to 90 percent of the current flow time in a straight polarity mode with the switching from straight-to-reverse polarity occurring at 41 to 46 cycles per second; or the straight polarity current flow should be 19 to 22 milliseconds and the reverse should be 2 to 4 milliseconds with a continuous switching between straight and reverse polarities during the welding operation.

Other Welding Variables. Many other variables affected the ability to weld consistently: torch angle, wire feed angle, electrode tip configuration, electrode centering, orifice diameter, orifice and shield gases, etc.

The most difficult variables to control were associated with the internal configuration of the torch. Variations in torch components affected orifice gases and shielding gases; or torch water cooling or improper electrode centering would negate established weld procedures if those variations were not carefully controlled. The torch component tolerances shown in Fig. 9 were necessary for process control.

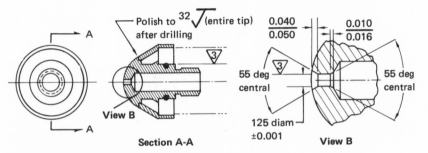

Notes:
1. All dimensions in inches.
2. Use silicon grease in assembling.
3. ⟨3⟩ concentric within 0.001 T.I.R.

Fig. 9 – Critical torch tolerances

Centering of the electrode was the most important factor in assuring proper torch functioning. Through this date, centering of the electrode has been largely dependent upon the skill of the individual assembling or maintaining the torch.

To ensure torch components and assembly were actually within tolerances, conformance tests were conducted by welding on test samples after any changes.

X-ray Anomalies

X-ray quality of keyhole plasma arc welded aluminum consistently showed defect rates of less than 0.5 percent. During process development, x-rays would often show anomalies difficult to differentiate from defects. The anomalies, typically shown in Fig. 10, probably were caused by diffraction of the x-rays from preferentially oriented grains in the weld metal. The anomalies were eliminated by using slightly higher heat inputs to the weld. Tensile property data indicated the anomalies had no mechanical effects on the welds (see Table 3), but anomaly elimination avoided any confusion in x-ray evaluation.

Generally, as-welded plasma arc mechanical properties are the same as annealed properties of the base metal.

Fig. 10 – Typical x-ray anomaly

Table 3
Typical as-welded mechanical properties of 5456 aluminum

X-ray quality of 5456-H116 welds	Yield strength, ksi	MPa	Ultimate strength, ksi	MPa	Elongation percentage for 2 in. (50 mm)
With x-ray anomalies	19.8	137	41.9	289	11.0
	21.7	150	44.5	307	14.0
	21.0	145	46.6	321	17.0
	21.8	150	46.2	319	15.0
	22.6	156	47.1	325	16.0
	21.8	150	46.8	323	16.0
Average	21.5	148	45.5	314	14.8
Clear	19.8	137	43.7	301	14.0
	21.5	148	45.5	314	15.0
	21.2	146	46.8	323	16.0
	21.3	147	46.0	317	15.0
	21.6	149	45.6	314	12.0
	21.2	146	43.3	299	12.0
	21.9	151	47.2	326	18.0
Average	21.2	146	45.4	313	14.6

Shrinkage

Free-state transverse weld shrinkage was measured on various thicknesses of keyhole plasma arc welded aluminum. The typical shrinkage from plasma welding was found to average 40 to 60 percent less than the shrinkage experienced in gas metal arc welding.

Welding Plates of Cast-to-Wrought Aluminum

A cast plate of A-356 was welded to a wrought plate of 5086. The resultant welds, when tested, failed in the heat-affected zone of the cast plate, as was expected.

Welding procedures for these dissimilar alloys and forms were easily established simply by using those procedures developed for the wrought material.

Out-of-Position Welding

Out-of-position welding was also done in wrought-to-wrought, cast-to-cast, and wrought-to-cast plates.

In general, top bead underfill at the upper edge of horizontal joints was minimized by elevating the wire feed guide tube to the upper leg of the weld pool and pointing into the pool from approximately 30° above horizontal.

Vertical joints were welded with various work and torch angles, which were dependent upon the work thicknesses. The maximum thickness achieved in vertical-up welding was 5/8 inch (15.8 mm). This thickness was a limit obtained with the available 300 amp power source and more power should have allowed greater thicknesses to be welded in the vertical position.

Summary

Plasma arc welding of aluminum in the keyhole mode has been accomplished using a variable polarity power source with independent amperage and time controls of the reverse and straight polarities. The basic welding variables require a higher reverse polarity amperage than for straight polarity, with a cyclic straight-to-reverse polarity switching at a millisecond ratio of approximately 20:3. The molten aluminum flows around and behind the keyhole plasma arc and then heals the joint, which has been locally cleaned of oxides by the bursts of reverse polarity current.

The process has been developed and is established as a reliable production method. Resultant welds are of high quality, exhibiting lower defect rates and less distortion than the familiar production weld techniques.

Acknowledgement

The authors wish to express their appreciation to H.W. Frye for his welding skills and suggestions that contributed significantly to the development and production implementation of keyhole plasma arc welding aluminum.

References

1. S.A. Nekrasov, G.P. Salking, et al. 1976. Employment of plasma arc welding in the manufacture of cryogenic equipment made of aluminum alloys. *Welding Production* 23(4): 16-17.

2. D.A. Dudko, et al. 1975. Thermal characteristics of a freely burning reversed polarity arc in the nonconsumable electrode welding for thin sheets of aluminum alloys. *Automatic Welding* 28(6): 1-3.

3. G.N. Kotov, et al. 1975. The influence of process conditions on the dimensions of the zones of cathodic cleaning in the welding of aluminum alloys. *Welding Production* 22(9): 45-47.

Welding for Low-Cost Advanced Titanium Airframe Structures

R.W. Messler, Jr. and C.A. Paez
Grumman Aerospace Corporation

While advanced processing technologies are currently the rage in attempting to improve the material utilization and to reduce the labor intensity associated with traditionally fabricated titanium airframes, hindsight shows that conventional technologies such as welding can play an even more versatile and valuable role than in the past.

The cost of fabricating titanium airframe structures by conventional aerospace manufacturing processes has traditionally been driven by two major factors: material utilization (or buy-to-fly ratio) and assembly labor intensity. While these factors are present with all aerospace materials, they are of particular concern with alloys that are inherently expensive and difficult to fabricate, as exemplified by titanium. Despite these difficulties, titanium alloys remain attractive for aerospace structural applications because of their high specific strength, modulus, and toughness; exceptional corrosion and fatigue resistance; high-temperature serviceability; and compatibility with other light-weight materials such as advanced organic matrix composites. For these reasons, government and industry have focused on overcoming the major cost drivers by developing advanced technologies, including superplastic forming with or without diffusion bonding (SPF/DB or SPF), hot isostatic pressing (HIP) of metal powders, casting, and isothermal forging and rolling. The goal is to build up titanium structures from fewer parts, with fewer fasteners, and with less material waste. Welding, although often overlooked, represents an ideal and widely available joining technique for many airframe structures.

By building up structures from detail parts using welding, overall structural efficiency and material utilization are often improved at the same time that labor-intensive assembly operations, such as mechanical fastening, are reduced or eliminated. By combining welding with the emerging advanced titanium processing technologies, other advantages are derived: detail part cost and weight are reduced (i.e., they are near-net-shape, unitized structures), overall structural size is not limited by available equipment capacity for a particular process (i.e., details can be joined together efficiently to produce larger assemblies), and structural optimization can be achieved by mixing and matching details fabricated by different processes into a hybrid structural assembly. An adjunct of welding as a means of building up low-cost, advanced titanium airframe structures is the reduction or offsetting of long lead times for titanium raw products or intermediate product forms like forgings.

Structural Efficiency

The variable geometry swing-wing of the F-14A fighter (see Fig. 1) requires that a wing center section (WCS) support the outer wing panels (see Fig. 2). These outer panels transmit large, variable bending and torsional moments as the wing is swept back and forth. Since the wing is located at the maximum cross-sectional area of the aircraft, aerodynamic considerations such as drag, area rule, etc., required that the wing box follow air passage contours. The resulting WCS is a 22-ft-long, gull-wing-shaped closed box that serves both as an integral fuel tank and a primary structural member (see Fig. 3).

Fig. 1 – F-14 Tomcats in flight showing fully swept and extended swing-wing capability

The fabrication approach for the WCS was extremely challenging. Since it was to be the structural heart of the aircraft to which the fuselage, nacelles, and outer wings were to be attached, dimensional accuracy and control, as well as strength and rigidity, were of paramount importance. Bolting would have produced severe weight and space problems. Minimal structural weight, high joint strength and efficiency, fracture toughness control, and leak-tightness all suggested welding as a primary fabrication joining process; and titanium alloys appeared an ideal material choice.

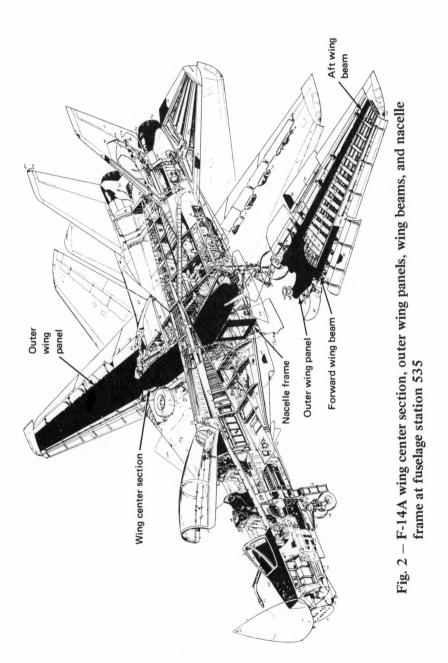

Fig. 2 – F-14A wing center section, outer wing panels, wing beams, and nacelle frame at fuselage station 535

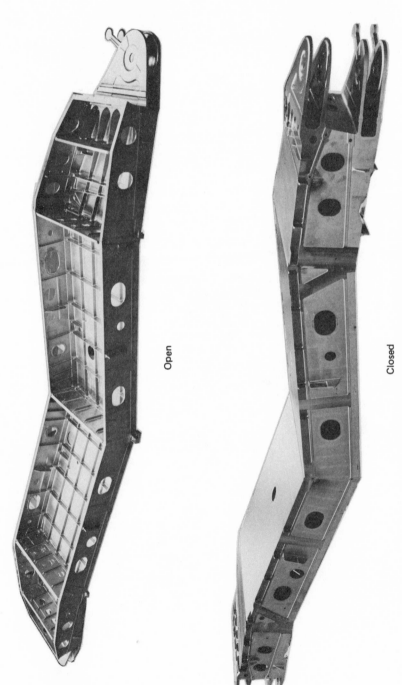

Open

Closed

Fig. 3 — F-14A all-titanium EB welded wing center section

In production, the F-14 WCS is fabricated by electron beam (EB) welding of Ti-6Al-4V machined detail parts. The resulting assembly is a unitized, monolithic structure. Seventy EB welds join over 33 detailed machined parts (see Fig. 4). Weld thicknesses range from 1/2 to over 2 in., and the total welded length exceeds 2200 inches. Fifty-seven welds are square butt joints, and 13 are angles or scarf joints; all are made in a single pass with no filler metal addition. Weld width is optimized to minimize shrinkage and distortion, while simultaneously minimizing the likelihood of missed seams or other weld defects.

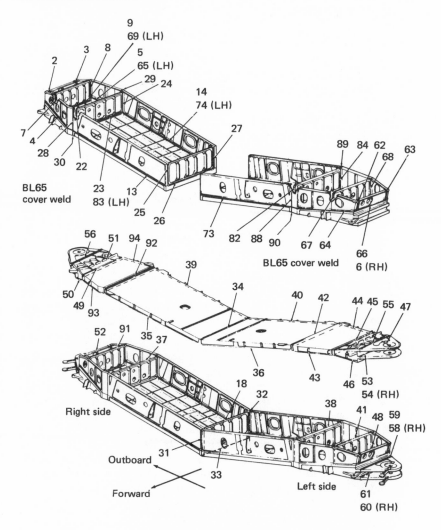

Fig. 4 – F-14A wing-center-section EB weld locations

By applying welding on the F-14 WCS, the following advantages were realized:

(1)   Labor intensity required to join the details was minimized.

(2)   Weight and stress concentrations were minimized by eliminating fasteners and the associated material required for obtaining high joint efficiency.

(3)   Structural efficiency, dimensional stability, and leak-tightness were maximized.

By employing EB welding in particular:

(1)   Weld quality and dimension control were maximized.

(2)   Joint static and fatigue strength efficiencies were maximized.

(3)   Welding labor intensity (due to single pass and high welding travel speeds) and consumables (no filler or inert gas) were minimized.

In summary, by building up the F-14 WCS from finished machined details by welding, structural efficiency was maximized, while labor intensity was kept to a minimum. If the same structure were to be redesigned and fabricated today, using the emerging near-net-shape structure processes (e.g., isothermal forging or isostatic pressing of metal powders in lieu of the conventional forging employed in the past), even further economies in material and machining could be achieved.

Improving Material Utilization

Due to the lug design requirements for the F-14A swing-wing fighter, EB welding was utilized to minimize material waste. The wing outer panel (Figs. 2 and 3) has a rather thick (1.5 in.) lug on the inboard end tapering down to a thin, pocketed plate (0.080 in.) on the outboard end. Although the original design had considered a bolted splice, EB welding was found to be a more economical, lighter, and more practical approach.

In the EB welded design, the lugs were designed to be machined from conventional forgings, while the skin was made from two machined plates (see Fig. 5). EB welding was used to join these machined parts. A short weld joined the lug to the small plate. This subassembly, was subsequently joined to the large plate by a 65-in.-long electron beam weld (5/8 in. maximum thickness) in a single pass. EB welding eliminated not only a difficult fuel sealing problem using mechanical fasteners, but also the associated stress concentrations and cost associated with a close-tolerance bolted joint. As an added bonus, the aircraft cross-sectional area was kept to a minimum, because the bolted splice would have added area and disturbed a critical contour location in the aircraft.

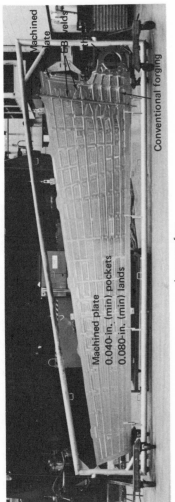

Fig. 5 — F-14A wing outer panel construction.

It should be noted that this is a 1969 design, but if this wing were to be designed today, welding would still be used. However, instead of joining machined plates, machined near-net-forged pivot fittings would be joined to welded SPF/DB wing cover sections. SPF/DB would not only further improve the material buy-to-fly ratio, but also eliminate over 5000 fasteners per wing; the associated cost of the fasteners, hole drilling, countersinking, and installation; and potential leak paths. In addition, many costly hot-formed detail parts and stiffeners would also be eliminated by the unitized construction made possible by SPF/DB (see Fig. 6).

Another example of using welding to improve material utilization is found in the F-14 wing beams. The F-14 outer wing panels consist of stringer-stiffened upper and lower covers joined at the leading and trailing edges by tapered-channel closure beams (see Fig. 2). Each beam, in fact, consists of a 9 ft outboard section and a 15 ft inboard section. The outboard aft beam originally was fabricated from a machined Ti-6Al-6V-2Sn (Ti-6-6-2) forging. The as-forged preform weighed 220 lb; following machining, the finished tapered channel weighed only 18 lb. The buy-to-fly ratio was nearly 12:1, and the lead time for forgings exceeded 100 weeks.

To improve the buy-to-fly ratio and alleviate the lead time problem, EB welding was again employed. L-shaped Ti-6-6-2 extrusions weighing 55 lb per pair were substituted for the original forging, thus reducing the buy-to-fly ratio to 3:1. Following a simple machining cut to taper the bottom leg of each extrusion, a tapered channel was produced by joining the extrusions with a single-pass EB weld the full length of the beam (see Fig. 7).

The resulting built-up beam had a 100 percent joint tensile efficiency across the EB weld. Although the beam was a fatigue-critical structure, the fatigue strength of the EB weld was of no consideration because the weld coincided with the beam's neutral axis. The improvement in buy-to-fly ratio resulted in reduced raw material cost and reduced machining labor. Lead time was shortened from 100 weeks for forgings to 24 to 32 weeks for extrusions. At the same time, beam structural performance was comparable to the original machined forging.

Increasing Processing Capability

Many of the near-net-shape processing technologies that offer improved material utilization are sensitive to component size. Either available facilities are size-limited, such as the high-temperature, high-pressure autoclave capacity available for hot isostatic processing of metal powders; or tooling costs become prohibitive as part plan-area increases, as with isothermal or hot die forging. Welding offers a low-cost means of efficiently joining near-net-shape details to overcome these size limitations. As a result, facility throughput can be increased by permitting efficient loading or nesting of smaller details, component size can be increased by building up details, and overall tooling costs can be kept to a practical minimum.

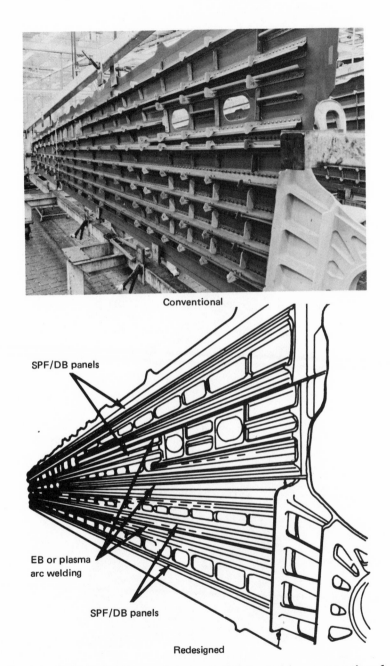

Fig. 6 — F-14A titanium wing cover fabricated by conventional methods and redesigned for SPF/DB and welding

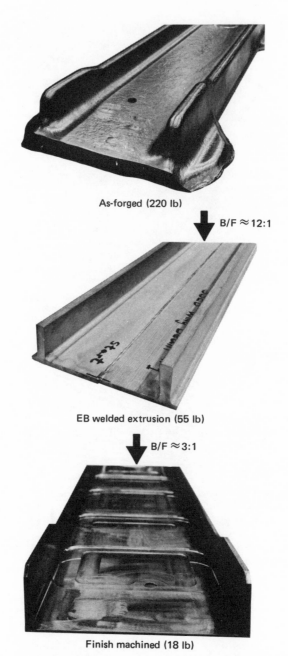

As-forged (220 lb)

B/F ≈ 12:1

EB welded extrusion (55 lb)

B/F ≈ 3:1

Finish machined (18 lb)

Fig. 7 – F-14A wing beams fabricated from machined forging and from machined, EB welded, built-up extrusions

An example is the nacelle frame at Fuselage Station 535 on the F-14 (see Fig. 2). Currently, this frame is fabricated from a Ti-6Al-4V (Ti-6-4) forging approximately 40-in. wide by 48-in. high, weighing 315 lb. Following machining, the finished frame weighs only 53 lb. To improve the material utilization (i.e., reduce the buy-to-fly ratio), hot isostatic pressing of Ti-6-4 powder has been proposed. Hot isostatically pressed Ti-6-6-2 alloy powder had already been shown to offer improved material utilization and equivalent properties compared to conventional forgings on a small brace in the WCS (see Fig. 8). However, due to the size and geometry of the nacelle frame, autoclave loading (even for the largest commercial facilities, which are 4 ft in diameter and 10 ft high) is inefficient with only two frames able to be processed in a single run. By breaking the frame into four nearly straight elements, part-packing efficiency in the autoclave is drastically improved, with elements for 10 frames per run possible (see Fig. 9). Per-unit cost and autoclave throughput are thus substantially improved. To produce the full nacelle frame, the four frame elements are EB welded together (see Fig. 10). Weld locations are selected to coincide with low ending-moment locations whenever possible.

Structural Optimization

A logical evolution of welding as a means for building up low-cost advanced titanium airframe structures is to blend structural details, fabricated by different processing techniques, to optimize the overall structure. An example is the all-titanium aft fuselage section of a conceptual tactical fighter studied in a recent US Air Force funded program called BLATS (Built-up Low-cost Advanced Titanium Structures). This program studied the value of combining innovative design concepts with advanced processing technologies, such as superplastic forming with concurrent diffusion bonding for built-up sheet-metal structures, and hot isostatic pressing for near-net-shape heavy sections. Traditionally machined plate/forged parts and built-up sheet-metal assemblies were evaluated using these innovative design concepts to attempt to minimize material cost, fabrication labor cost, and structural weight. Welding was used to join details into optimized blended/hybrid structural assemblies. A typical case is one of the fuselage bulkheads (see Fig. 11) in which the center portion of the bulkhead was designed as a two-sheet SPF/DB assembly. The lower frames were designed as one-sheet SPF parts, while the outer sections were designed as HIP parts. Welding was selected as the joining method to eliminate fasteners, their required holes, and potential fuel leak paths near the hot area adjacent to the engine.

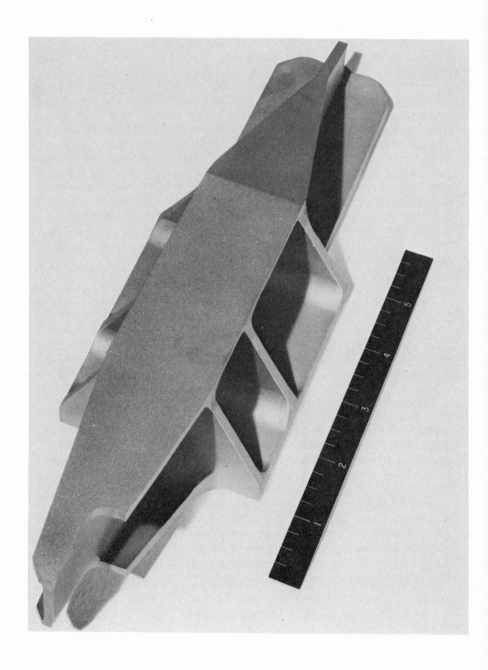

Fig. 8 – Hot isostatically pressed Ti-6Al-6V-2Sn fuselage brace

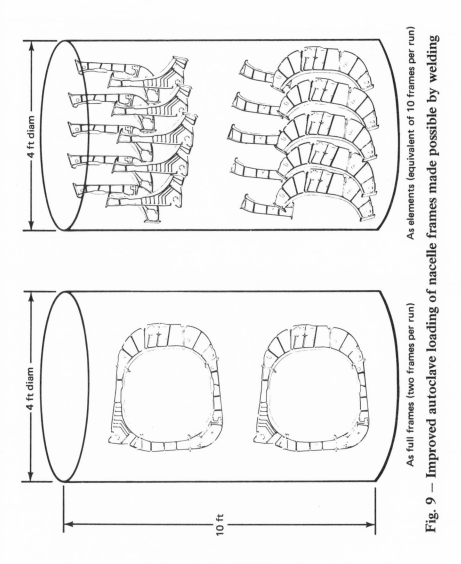

As full frames (two frames per run)

As elements (equivalent of 10 frames per run)

Fig. 9 — Improved autoclave loading of nacelle frames made possible by welding

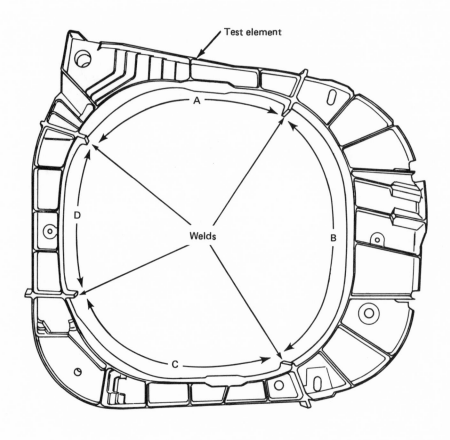

**Fig. 10 – Nacelle frame fabricated from EB welded
HIP'd elements**

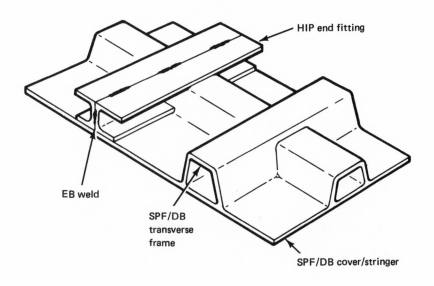

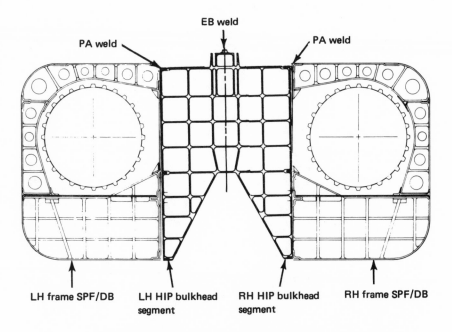

Fig. 11 — Hybrid bulkhead concept for advanced aircraft using welding to join SPF/DB, HIP, and isothermally forged details

Conclusions

Welding is clearly a valuable, versatile, and widely available technique for building up low-cost advanced titanium structures for modern airframes. It offers:

(1) Improved structural efficiency

(2) Improved material utilization

(3) Expanded near-net-shape processing capability

(4) Structural optimization

To be most beneficial, the welding processes employed should provide:

(1) High joint efficiencies for static and fatigue loading

(2) High quality

(3) Low distortion and shrinkage (especially when used to join finished or near-net-shaped details)

(4) High welding speeds or deposition rates to minimize welding labor intensity

Welding represents a conventional metal processing technology that can play an even more vital role in modern airframe fabrication.

Are Digital Arc Welding Programmers Suitable for the Aerospace Industry?

George J. Mueller
Merrick Engineering, Inc.

Welding engineers depend heavily on welding programmers. Most welding engineers are familiar with the arc welding programmer as a device to automate tube-to-tube welds. The welding programmer has to a large extent evolved in response to requirements of aerospace manufacturing. The welding programmer, especially in GTAW and PAW, has become perhaps a very sophisticated and specialized programmable controller. These instruments combine the functions of timing, logic, slope generation, variable pulsation and indication/readout. The programmer is often the heart of welding systems involving programmed current supplies, travel controls, wire feeders, arc voltage controls, and other subsystems needed for controlling some aspect of the welding process.

In recent years, advances of technology have permitted the replacement of large relay panels with the smaller, more efficient programmable control. A similar trend is likely to occur in the area of welding programmers. Many manufacturers will offer the newer digitally-based machines to replace instruments based on relays and operational amplifiers. It is worthwhile to make a comparison between the two technologies and attempt to determine the relative merits of each when applied to welding instrumentation. It is the intent of this paper to make a noncomprehensive, but informative, comparison between the two general approaches to help the welding engineer understand and evaluate welding programmer advances.

Human engineering is a relatively new technique used in designing equipment with the human operator in mind. As machinery becomes more complex in response to more stringent production requirements, design of the operator's control panels must be thoughtfully undertaken, with prime objectives being: (1) ease of functional understanding, (2) ease of information entry, (3) ease of information readout, and (4) ease in troubleshooting. Thought should also be given to how particular controls can be interfaced to a variety of equipment likely to be used in the same system, so that in the case of weld current programmer, it could become the central sequencing and parameter control for an entire automatic welding system.

If we look at the history of welding programmer panel layouts and use Miller/Merrick equipment as a sample, we can see how concepts have evolved in designing an operator's programmer panel.

Figure 1 shows the early 1960's version of a programmed GTAW power supply, the ESR-150. A close-up of the control panels, Fig. 2, shows how each timer and sloper function had its own module. One can also see the main current dial in the second panel, the only direct reading multiturn pot on the panel. While this approach may seem logical to the equipment designer, the resulting panel layout has little logical flow for the operator.

Integration of the weld programmer into one unit with dials and lights set into a graphic type display is accomplished in the Amptrak II, shown installed in the TCR-300 in Fig. 3. All time dials are across the bottom of the panel and read out directly in seconds, with sequential lighted push buttons above each one to indicate program progress. Current dials, all reading directly in amperes, are placed on the panel in a graph of a typical program, showing upslope and downslope. Pulsing controls are separate but are also multiturn pots and dials for direct readout. The front panel appears almost as one would graph the programmed current as a function of time. The operator has no difficulty in visualizing what he is controlling.

As the welding requirements for components such as nuclear fuel rod ends and small precision switches dictated a need for additional functions, the Amptrak V (see Fig. 4) evolved. An additional slope and an additional initial current timer were added. Digital thumbpots replaced the multiturn pots or dials for easier data entry.

As in the first Amptrak shown, all sloping functions are generated by two opposite-moving slope circuits, using operational amplifiers and integrating capacitors. Thus, any slope can be upward or downward, or by setting the current dials the same, the slope can be flat. If a requirement exists that a slope must be initiated by a position sensor (e.g., limit switch) or other external control, that capability is built in also. This enables the welding engineer to accurately coordinate the timed weld program with the speed of the moving part (or torch). This is particularly useful in tube welding, and where it is desirable to have the rotating device and the weld begin and end at the same point every time.

For the requirement where the speed of the moving part (or torch) must be varied during the program, a speed control such as the multispeed Orbit Arc programmer can be added, as shown in the second panel of the TXR-100 in Fig. 5. Since both programmers are analog timer-based, there is some difficulty in coordinating the functions of each. Nevertheless, the system as shown in Fig. 5 constitutes a complete tube welding machine, less head, and is used both in the laboratory and on the production floor because of its flexibility and reliability.

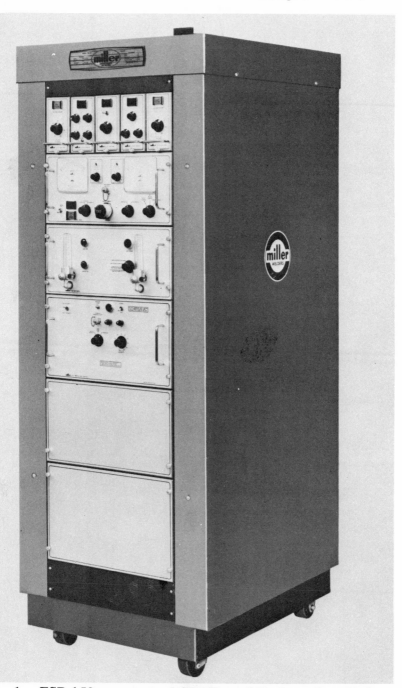

Fig. 1 — ESR-150 programmed GTAW machine from the 1960's

Fig. 2 — Close-up: ESR-150 control panel

Fig. 3 — TCR-300 with Amptrak II including pulser

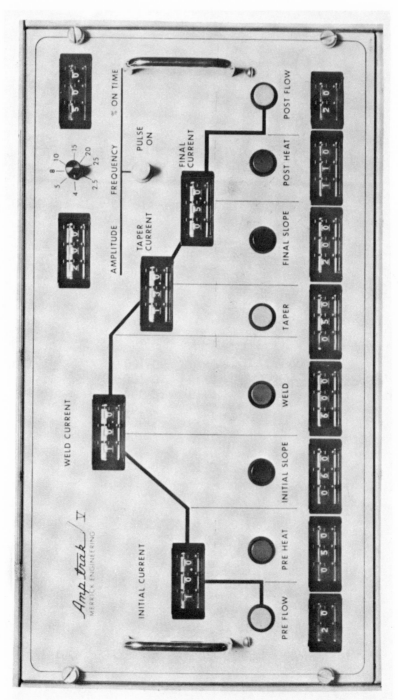

Fig. 4 – Amptrak V current programmer

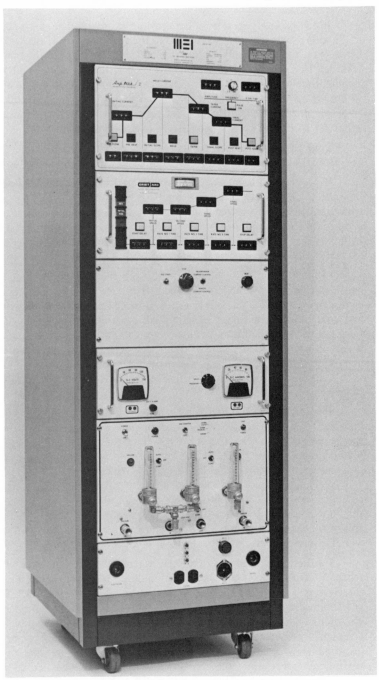

Fig. 5 — TXR-100 with Amptrak V and Orbit Arc 24

It can be easily seen from the previous examples that as the complexity of the weld programmer increases, due to the requirements of the weld profile, there is a point beyond which the addition of more dials is no longer feasible. The Amptrak VII shown in Fig. 6 with five slopes and two non-sloping timers, plus preflow and postflow, approaches a physical limit as to how many functions will fit on a front panel. The possibility of operator error in setting this multiplicity of controls is another consideration. So where does this lead us, this progression of programmers?

Let's return to what is being sought in a welding programmer. What are the user, the welding engineer, and the operator on the floor looking for?

We begin with human compatibility and discovered the possibilities and limitations of dial-set analog programmers. Newer digital-based programmers, which still use front panel switches for welding variables data entry, are admittedly more accurate; however, the limitations in flexibility still apply. In fact, many new digital programmers limit their slope generating capability and offer multiple step current functions instead.

Compatibility with other controls in the welding system is also a consideration, as previously mentioned. If the weld programmer is the nerve center for a GTAW welding setup, then it must have provision for sequencing and controlling such things as wire feed, arc voltage, and speed of part (or torch) motion. While this was seen to be possible with the analog programmer, it was also noted that because of timer accuracies, consistent synchronization of multiple timing functions is not really feasible. Digital-based programmers, with crystal controlled or line frequency derived clock-timers, eliminate this problem.

Flexibility, or the ability to use the welding machine for a variety of precision parts, is another consideration. One type of part may require a simple programmer like the Amptrak II (see Fig. 3), while another weld requires the multiple slopes of the Amptrak VII and at the same time a speed program of the Orbit Arc (Figs. 5 and 6). While the complex programmers will surely do the work of the simple one, it sometimes leads to frustration and confusion to have to enter values that are not required for the part but that are required to make the welding machine sequence properly. The ability to change the format to suit the complexity of the part weldment would surely be appreciated by engineer and operator alike.

Furthermore, while an extremely versatile machine may be well suited for the lab environment and very useful in developing variables and techniques for welding a new part, what happens when it comes time for production, and the machine cannot withstand the often hostile industrial environment? The older type of programmer and power supply, having been designed using techniques and components that were not very susceptible to dirty air or high-frequency noise, performed satisfactorily in the welding production environment. But while these analog machines are reliable and rugged, they appear to have reached their limit in the other areas. Again, where does that lead us?

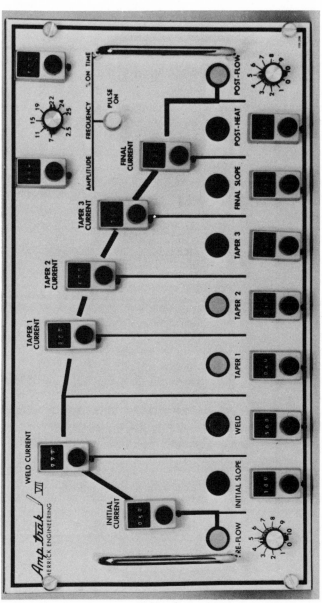

Fig. 6 – Amptrak VII

What if the ruggedness and noise immunity of the analog approach were combined with the nearly limitless flexibility of the digital approach? Would this not be the best of both worlds?

Let's examine some of the features available when a weld programmer goes digital, and let's examine some of the methods used in going digital and what trade-offs there are in each.

One method we touched on before is using digital switches to enter the variables. Digital timers whose base is the line frequency can have accuracies to within one-half cycle or 8.4 milliseconds. Crystal-controlled clocks can be even more accurate and have the advantage of not needing to select 50 or 60 Hz operation. (This is an advantage both for the manufacturer and the multinational user.) Digital current setting, using D/A converters, is also very accurate. Many truly digital programmers, however, only step between current functions, as the process of digital slope generation is fairly complex. This is particularly so when combined with proportional pulsing. Therefore, while this type of digital programmer is accurate, its flexibility is still limited by the number of dials on the panel. Because variables are entered directly on the dials, it is not possible to interface the programmer directly to a central computer, as might also be desirable.

How can the digital instrument capitalize on its inherent flexibility? How can it free itself from the bonds of direct-dial data entry? And how can it maintain the ease of data entry and operator understanding that go with graphic front panels?

One answer is to use digital memory to store variables; use a large CRT screen to read out those variables; and enter the data on a keyboard. Then design the entire instrument to allow the operator all the flexibility and easy interfacing possible with that instrument. Such a system is the Amptrak Micro. A crystal-controlled clock maintains time and pulse accuracies to within 0.02 seconds over each interval's range of 0.1 to 999.9 seconds. The number of intervals is selectable from 1 to 14, plus preflow and postflow. Each interval is normally sloped; however, if external triggers are used to end one interval and begin another, the current (or speed) will step from one level to another. The system is two-channel: Normally one channel controls the weld current output of a constant current GTAW supply; the second channel controls the speed of a positioning device, such as a tube-to-tube head. For those functions that do not require an analog control voltage such as start and stop of carriage, oscillator, etc., an open collector transistor output switches on during each of the 14 intervals. Several units can be ganged together, forming a completely coordinated control center for welding, such as will include arc voltage control and wire feed.

Each of the two channel can be pulsed together, and each interval can have a different pulse frequency and percent on-time. As one quickly sees, the program can be as simple or as complex as one can practically desire. *Flexibility.*

But where is the graphic display? How does the operator keep track of where the sequence is and how can he change values during a weld?

Fourteen intervals, with all the information for each one, as shown in Fig. 7, couldn't be displayed in the usual graphic fashion. But the information arranged in tabular form here affords a view of the entire program. Furthermore, as the program proceeds, the interval in progress is highlighted by reverse video (note line 6 in Fig. 7). Also, the time and current and speed data are all updated at a one-second rate to show the progress of that interval. Time times down, while current and speed slope between their end point values. Total elapsed time is also displayed as the program is proceeding.

If the operator wishes to trim the current (or speed) up or down, he can do so in 3 percent increments (or decrements) by using the arrow keys on the keyboard. The changes made are retained in the program without further action. Any unusual occurrences during a sequence, such as an emergency stop or program adjustment, are noted on the screen at the end of the sequence. And for a permanent written record of the program, a printer with an RS232 connector may be attached. If desired, a printout of the program will occur at the end of each completed sequence. *Flexibility and adaptability.*

How about entry and storage of variables data? When the programmer is first powered up and accessed, it asks the operator how complex his program is. Once that format is selected, the programmer reverse video highlights each data space and waits for the operator to key in the variable. Pressing CONT (continue) moves the "cursor" to the next data space, and the operator continues to fill out the program until all spaces are full. Before pushing CONT a final time, data can be changed by using the arrow keys to move the arrow to the space in question. When the machine is ready, it says so, and the operator may push "sequence start."

To prevent unauthorized personnel from operating this welding programmer, the first question asked upon power-up is, "What is the authorization code?" Without entering this 4-digit number, no further access is possible, and depressing the keys has no effect. The programmer may also be set for "no code required," if desired.

In the development of a process, this program may be used and altered as required. To store it for later use, no additional equipment is needed. One uvpROM will store up to eight programs, and can be programmed (burned in) directly by the Amptrak. The pROM can be erased and reused, and additional "memory cartridges," each containing one of these memory chips, can be obtained and used. Multiple programs of wide variety can be stored. The flexibility is available for laboratory work in developing weld schedules.

Now it comes time to go into production. Will this digital programmer stand up?

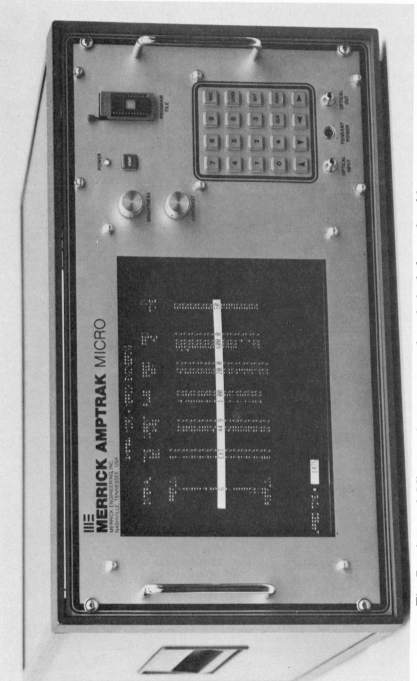

Fig. 7 – Amptrak Micro - microprocessor-based, dual channel weld programmer

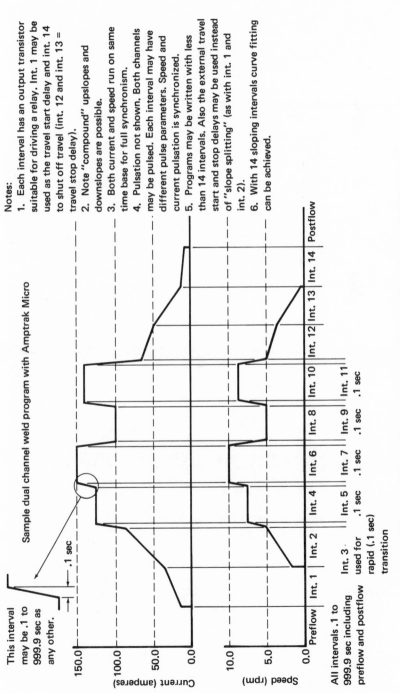

Notes:

1. Each interval has an output transistor suitable for driving a relay. Int. 1 may be used as the travel start delay and int. 14 to shut off travel (int. 12 and int. 13 = travel stop delay).

2. Note "compound" upslopes and downslopes are possible.

3. Both current and speed run on same time base for full synchronism.

4. Pulsation not shown. Both channels may be pulsed. Each interval may have different pulse parameters. Speed and current pulsation is synchronized.

5. Programs may be written with less than 14 intervals. Also the external travel start and stop delays may be used instead of "slope splitting" (as with int. 1 and int. 2).

6. With 14 sloping intervals curve fitting can be achieved.

Sample dual channel weld program with Amptrak Micro

This interval may be .1 to 999.9 sec as any other.

.1 sec

150.0

100.0

50.0

0.0

Current (amperes)

10.0

5.0

0.0

Speed (rpm)

All intervals .1 to 999.9 sec including preflow and postflow

| Preflow | Int. 1 | Int. 2 | Int. 3 used for rapid (.1 sec) transition | Int. 4 | Int. 5 .1 sec | Int. 6 | Int. 7 .1 sec | Int. 8 | Int. 9 .1 sec | Int. 10 | Int. 11 .1 sec | Int. 12 | Int. 13 | Int. 14 | Postflow |

Fig. 8 – Typical program generation using Amptrak Micro

At the outset of this product design, much attention was given to the elimination of noise interference, especially noise generated by the high-frequency arc starter. The typical high-frequency generator has a spark gap oscillator operating around one or two megahertz and several thousand volts. This energy propogates to the arc, and also through the air, back through the power lines, and back to the work and electrode connections of the power source. All lines that feed the arc starter are filtered to prevent the noise from ever entering the cabinet that contains the power source and programmer. The "computer box," the assembly that contains the microprocessor boards and all digital circuitry, is fabricated with a machined aluminum outer case. All digital (on/off) electrical signals that go in or out of this box do so via feed-through capacitors and ferrite bead filters, and they are also optically isolated. Operator keyboard and program memory chip mount directly to one side of the computer box. The CRT used is a heavy-duty industrial type. The only direct signal paths between the instrument and the outside world are the two analog output drive signals. These are carefully filtered to keep out high-frequency noise.

Care was taken also in the grounding system to ensure that noise was not introduced via that path. The result is a programmer that has been demonstrated to be well protected against electrical noise interference.

Besides the weld programmer itself, which is usually a large instrument itself or is actually integrated into a power supply, a pendant is usually required for certain remote operations. The typical pendant is a rather bulky, heavy affair, with digital switches, push buttons and lights, and a thick pendant cable.

All these disadvantages can be eliminated with a computer-based programmer. The pendant shown in Fig. 9 has a fiber optic cable for digital information, plus a power pair for the display. Display is selectable from any of the key parameters on the CRT, and any of the current or speed levels can be adjusted while welding. Four user-selectable jog buttons are available also, as well as "start," "continue," and "stop." And all this is contained in a package the size of a hand-held calculator, capable of being carried almost anywhere.

To summarize and to answer the question that is the title of this presentation: Yes, digital welding programmers are here, and *especially* for the aerospace industry, with its critical standards of reliability, accuracy, and flexibility needs, they are now particularly well suited. We have looked at various trade-offs made in going digital, pointing out the benefits and drawbacks of each. Now the welding engineer and equipment buyer must study the various options, weigh the costs and benefits, look at the needs, and select the unit that will work for the company now and in the future, in the lab and in production.

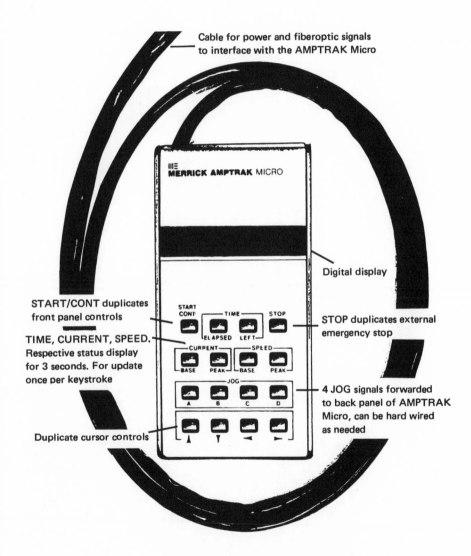

Cable for power and fiberoptic signals to interface with the AMPTRAK Micro

Digital display

START/CONT duplicates front panel controls

STOP duplicates external emergency stop

TIME, CURRENT, SPEED. Respective status display for 3 seconds. For update once per keystroke

4 JOG signals forwarded to back panel of AMPTRAK Micro, can be hard wired as needed

Duplicate cursor controls

Fig. 9 — Pendant for remote control of Amptrak[R] Micro weld programmer

The Application of Fracture Control to a Weld Specification

D.A. Bolstad, L.W. Loechel, and F.R. Clover
Martin Marietta

Introduction

In general, the acceptance of defects in typical aerospace welding specifications is very conservative. The acceptance of defects, such as cracks, inclusions, or lack-of-fusion, is, in fact, almost unheard of in man-rated vehicles. The purpose of this paper is to describe the approach used on the external tank (ET) portion of the Space Shuttle Program, which uses fracture control to establish defect acceptance criteria in a welding specification. In addition, the method in which weld properties affect the proof test conditions will be discussed.

Background

A schematic of the ET is shown in Fig. 1. The ET is 153.7 feet (46.8 m) long with a diameter of 27.6 feet (8.4 m). The purpose of the ET is to provide propellants to the main shuttle engines located in the Orbiter. The ET is composed essentially of two propellant tanks, a large liquid hydrogen tank and a smaller liquid oxygen tank, joined together by an intertank to form one large propellant storage container. Both the hydrogen and oxygen tanks are welded pressure vessels. The hydrogen tank contains approximately 24,000 inches of weld, while the oxygen tank contains approximately 12,000 inches of weld.

The alloy from which the ET is fabricated is 2219 aluminum. Table 1 gives the composition range for the alloy.

---

1. This work sponsored by the NASA Marshall Space Flight Center, Alabama, under Contract No. NAS8-30300.

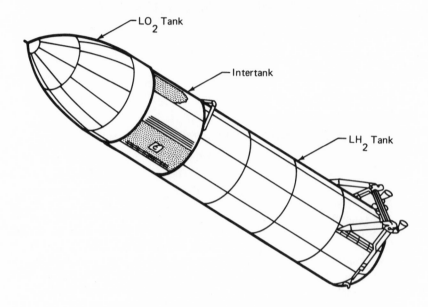

Fig. 1 — The external tank

Table 1
Composition range for 2219 aluminum

Copper	5.8-6.8	Zinc	0.10 max
Manganese	0.2-0.4	Magnesium	0.02 max
Iron	0.30 max	Vanadium	0.05-0.015
Silicone	0.20 max	Zirconium	0.10-0.25
Titanium	0.02-0.10	Other	0.05 each
Al	Balance	Other	Total 0.15 max

2219 was selected for several reasons: (1) good weld strength at room temperature (typical 42,000 psi), (2) increasing strength at cryogenic temperatures (liquid hydrogen at −423° F and liquid oxygen at −293° F), (3) increasing fracture toughness with cryogenic temperatures, and (4) good weldability. The good weldability statement results from 2219's lack of crack propagation during welding and the ability to weld repair 2219 a number of times without degrading the properties.

The welding on the ET is accomplished in three passes: a seal pass, a penetration pass, and a fill pass using 2319 weld wire. 2319 has essentially the same composition as 2219. See Ref. 1 for a much more detailed description of the ET welding processes and tooling.

Requirements

Contracturally, the ET was required to survive without failure for at least 4 mission cycles and to account for the presence of cracks or crack-like defects (fracture control) in the design. Translated into practice, this meant that the ET welding specification could allow cracks or crack-like defects to remain in the structure as long as the mission requirements could be met. Past experience with fracture control in the aerospace industry has frequently been associated with high costs, caused mainly by special inspection techniques. Therefore, any acceptance of defects had to be within the reliable capability of the ET weld inspection techniques for x-ray penetrant inspection.

Technical Approach

When allowing for the presence of cracks or crack-like defects in a structure, the engineer must consider three modes of failure:

(1) *Static overload* – The initial flaw size exceeds the critical flaw size during the proof test or during flight.

(2) *Sustained flaw growth* – A less-than-critical flaw grows during an extended period of loading to a critical size. This flaw growth can be accelerated by an aggressive environment. For the ET, sustained stresses can occur during proof test, during storage (if stored with positive pressure), and during the flight itself.

(3) *Cyclic flaw growth* – The flaw grows to a critical size due to pressurization cycles for leak checks, propellant loadings, and/ or flight.

An empirical approach was selected for generation of fracture behavior data. Specimen thicknesses, flaw sizes, and loading profiles for flaw growth evaluations were all selected to simulate those of the ET. With this approach, the question of the validity of application of linear elastic analyses to a tough material like 2219 was avoided; data was developed for simulated service conditions.

Test Procedure and Analysis

The test specimens were prepared with known cracks. The cracks were introduced by electrical discharge machining a slot and extending the slot by fatigue cycles. By trial and error, the slot shape and fatigue loading can be adjusted to produce a pre-existing crack of known configuration. Then, this specimen with a crack is exposed to a known load environment or load cycles and the flaw growth behavior or fracture strength is determined.

Figure 2 is a plot of fracture strength for typical 2219 welds with a flaw in the weld centerline. Using these data, the designer can predict the failure stress for differing size flaws. The a/2c ratio describes the shape of the flaw, where a is the crack depth and 2c is the crack length.

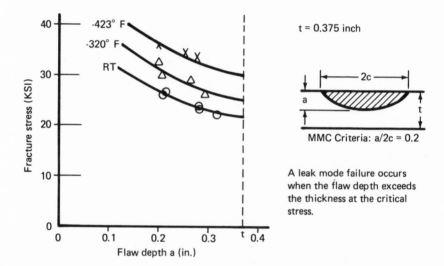

Fig. 2 – Flaw depth versus fracture strength for 2219-T87 welds

Most of the flaws tested in this program were semi-elliptical (a/2 = 0.2) in shape, as this best approximated weld defects. Note in Fig. 2 that 2219 gets "tougher" with colder temperature; for an identical flaw, the fracture stress increases with decreasing temperatures. Reference 2 is a more detailed report on the 2219 fracture test results and test procedures used on the ET program.

Application

The empirical fracture tests resulted in three applications to ET welds:

(1) Determination of the proof factor

(2) Weld acceptance criteria in the welding specification

(3) Leak-before-burst design

Proof Factor. The purpose of a proof test is to test an article at a stress intensity higher than operational to assure that the article will survive the operational life. For short-life applications, a proof factor of 1.05 is generally sufficient. Starting at this point of reference, the ET proof tests are also designed to take advantage of the 2219 property of increased toughness at lower temperatures. Using the following formula, the proof factor for the ET was established:

$$\text{ET proof factor} = 1.05 \times \frac{\text{Toughness at ambient temperature}}{\text{Toughness at cryogenic temperature}}$$

At liquid oxygen temperatures, the toughness of 2219 welds are 5 percent higher than room temperature; thus, for the liquid oxygen tank, the proof factor is 1.00. For the liquid hydrogen tank, the proof factor is 0.955, due to the fact the toughness at $-423°$ F is 10 percent higher than ambient.

Weld Acceptance Criteria. Using ambient temperature data similar to Fig. 2 for the various ET weld thickness, the weld acceptance criteria for 2219 were developed in the following manner:

(1) Determine critical flaw depths at 20,000 psi, 25,000 psi, and 30,000 psi stress. This brackets the most critical stresses in the ET welds.

(2) Convert these flaw depths into flaw lengths by multiplying the depth by 5 (remember, $a/2c = 0.2$). This conversion is necessary because x-ray and penetrant inspection can only determine the flaw lengths.

(3) Divide the critical lengths by two. This is important, as this is the margin of safety to allow for uncertainties in the stress analysis and inaccuracies in the inspection techniques.

(4) Next consider a semicircular flaw where the flaw depth is equal to the thickness. This is a flaw that will leak. Compare this flaw length to the length determined above. Use whichever length is smallest.

(5) Round off the lengths to the nearest 0.05 inch to help the inspection.

The result of this approach is shown in Fig. 3. This graph is used by the design or stress engineers to determine the acceptable flaw size for each weld.

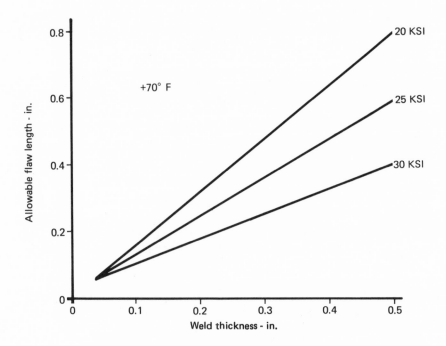

Fig. 3 — Weld defects allowable

In line with the practice of using grades to denote inspection level, the 2219 specification includes a table of weld grades as a function of acceptable defect length. Figure 4 contains the grades used on the ET program.

The design drawing specifies the weld grade for a particular weld; then the inspector uses the grade to determine the defect length for radiographic and penetrant acceptance of the weld.

Leak-before-burst design. This is a fairly new concept to welded pressure vessel designs. In summary, the approach is to limit weld stresses to a level such that the critical flaw depth at proof will be greater than the weld thickness. What this means in theory is that the weld will leak before it fractures or ruptures. Therefore, if inspection has missed a critical defect, there is the possibility that a leak can be detected visually before full proof pressure is attained. In practice, these leak-before-burst criteria create a design with larger critical flaws, and this in turns makes flaw detection much easier. A more detailed description of leak-before-burst design is found in Ref. 3. Where practical, ET welds were designed to be leak-before-burst.

Grade	Defect length (L) in.[1]
	MSFC-SPEC-504, para. 3.12 to 3.12.1.8 and 3.13.1
1	to 3.13.1.8 inclusive (Appendix A)
2	0.125 $L \leqslant 0.130$ (Inch)
3	$L \leqslant 0.140$
4	$L \leqslant 0.150$
5	$L \leqslant 0.200$
6	$L \leqslant 0.250$
7	$L \leqslant 0.300$
8	$L \leqslant 0.350$
9	$L \leqslant 0.400$
10	$L \leqslant 0.450$
11	$L \leqslant 0.500$
12	$L \leqslant 0.550$
13	$L \leqslant 0.600$
14	$L \leqslant 0.650$
15	$L \leqslant 0.700$
16	$L \leqslant 0.750$
17	$L \leqslant 0.800$
18	$L \leqslant 0.850$
19	$L \leqslant 0.900$
20	$L \leqslant 0.950$
21	$L \leqslant 1.000$

1. In no case shall the allowable defect length for a single defect exceed 1.8 t, where t = material thickness of thinnest member when the weld is a portion of a pressure vessel.

Fig. 4 – 2219-T87 weld grades

Design Example

To better understand the ET approach, one of the ET welds will be examined in more detail. The basic information is as follows:

(1) Weld number   HB3-4
(2) Weld thickness   0.340 in.
(3) Weld stress   20,000 psi

The stress engineer using Fig. 3 and the 20,000 stress values determines that the HB3-4 weld has an allowable defect of 0.540 inch. From the weld specification (Fig. 4), grade 11 is selected as the drawing callout. (Note, since 0.540 in. is less than the 0.550 in. maximum allowed under grade 12, the next lower grade [0.550 inch] is chosen.) The process planning paper next instructs quality control to inspect this weld to grade 11. This approach is repeated for all the ET welds. An important economic advantage of this approach is that one particular weld with tight requirements does not penalize all the rest of the welds, since acceptance criteria are established on an individual weld basis.

Summary

The success of the ET weld acceptance criteria is best seen from the success of the proof tests. To date, six test tanks and ten flight tanks have successfully passed proof test. In addition, the ET used in conjunction with the shuttle main engine tests has been pressured at least 12 times with a total operational time in excess of 44 minutes. The Shuttle flight itself is approximately 10 minutes.

Further evidence of the usefulness of the ET criteria is the acceptance of the approach by the weld engineers and welders. By allowing each weld to be judged by its own defect requirement instead of using the tightest requirement, the number of weld repairs has been minimized, resulting in lower cost with no compromise in performance.

References

1. Clover, F.R. 1980. Welding of the external tank of the space shuttle. *Welding Journal* 59(8).

2. Fiftal, C.F. 1975. Fracture mechanics data on 2219-T87 aluminum for the space shuttle external tank. *Martin Marietta Aerospace - Michoud Operation Test Report 826-2027.*

3. Bolstad, D.A. and Loechel, L.W. 1977. Application of fracture mechanics to welded structures design. *Case Studies in Fracture Mechanics* Army Materials and Mechanics Research Center.

Engineering Aspects of a Weld Repair Program

T.J. Bosworth, E.C. Arnaldo, F.J. Rooney, and A.W. Steele
Boeing Aerospace Company

Introduction

One of the most difficult welding programs to engineer involves the *in situ* repair or rework of existing operational structures. At first glance, the task appears to be no different than any other weld engineering job. Engineering drawings are available, weld process specifications and joint weld procedures must be prepared, and planning paper drafted. The quality control department must prepare its plans, material must be ordered, and the welding crews must be brought in and certified. A routine engineering job, right? Wrong!

The job soon grinds to a halt. The actual hardware is unlike the drawing, dimensions are off, welds are misplaced or oversized, electrical cables and piping runs that aren't shown on the initial structural drawings are in the way, residual stresses cause unending fit-up problems, and the volume of paper created by the engineering change orders soon obliterates the structure being repaired.

Analysis of the situation quickly reveals the source of the problem:

(1) Information on the repair of existing structures is virtually non-existent in industry welding codes or in the literature. Thus, engineers confronted with weld repair programs must establish their own guidelines.

(2) Weld process specifications must have an inherent, controlled flexibility written into them that addresses the highly variable conditions of the repair activity.

(3) Optional repair approaches must be established that will satisfy structural design requirements. These must be readily available to the welder so that work can proceed with minimum interruption.

The job is now re-evaluated, a new approach is established, new engineering is drafted, and, finally, the work gets under way. As work progresses and experience is gained, engineering changes to accommodate new problems give way to those that improve productivity and reduce cost.

This paper presents the authors' experience with a major weld repair program conducted at 50 Minuteman silos in north central Montana, involving the repair, upgrading, or replacement of approximately 1000 feet of weld joints at each site. It addresses the evolution of the engineering documentation and the results of the engineering effort and provides guidelines for conducting future programs of this type.

The Technical Problem

The Minuteman system, consisting of 1000 sites spread over eight western states, has been this country's first line of defense for nearly two decades. The sites are grouped in six wings of 150 to 200 sites each. Wing I in central Montana contains 200 sites, including a co-located squadron of 50 sites. As the system matured, the original missiles were replaced with larger and more powerful missiles (Minuteman II), which in turn were replaced with still larger and more powerful missiles (Minuteman III). While the basic envelopes of the silos did not change, internal structures were modified and strengthened, and new, more complex support systems were added. Simultaneous strengthening of the structures was required to ensure that the silos would withstand more powerful enemy threats. To accomplish these changes, the Minuteman program conducted as many as 10 modification programs at each site, in which structural elements were removed, replaced, strengthened, or reconfigured.

Originally, separate engineering drawings were prepared for each wing, but not for each site. Changes occurring during the construction or each modification of each site that were outside of an engineering "tolerance zone" were recorded as unplanned engineering events, which did not precipitate a change to the master drawings, but did, in effect, alter the configuration of the hardware. Many unplanned events were to take place at each site that were to have a significant impact on the weld repair activities.

In mid-1977, it was determined that the 50 co-located sites in north central Montana contained a number of weld joints with questionable weld quality that might not fulfill the original design requirement to survive a nuclear blast. Following detailed structural analysis of each weld joint and the forces acting on each structural element, it was determined that approximately 1000 feet of welded joints would be reworked, replaced, or strengthened in each silo. These included fillet and groove welds and combinations thereof, from several inches to over 30 feet in length, in ASTM A36 steel, ranging from 3/16 inch to over 2 inches in thickness.

To complicate the situation, repair activities were to be conducted with much of the supporting equipment in place; hence, elaborate protective coverings were to be installed over electronic gear. Additionally, many weld joints would be repaired under load, which meant that only part of the joint could be removed and replaced at any given time.

The Welding Environment

In Montana, the silos are scattered over broad areas of ranch land, often with many miles of gravel road between sites. The silos involved in this program were spread over an 80-mile circle centered approximately 70 miles due north of Great Falls. Temperatures range from the 90s in the summer to more than 20 below zero in the winter, and the chill factor from winter winds will drive the effective temperature to −50° F or below. Except for two welds about 1 foot long, all welding was below grade where excessive temperatures and wind were seldom a problem, although frozen flowmeters were not uncommon in the winter.

The silos are concrete and A36 steel structures approximately 90 feet deep and 13 feet in diameter in the lower and upper launch tubes (see Fig. 1). The launch equipment room is approximately 25 feet in diameter by about 20 feet high.

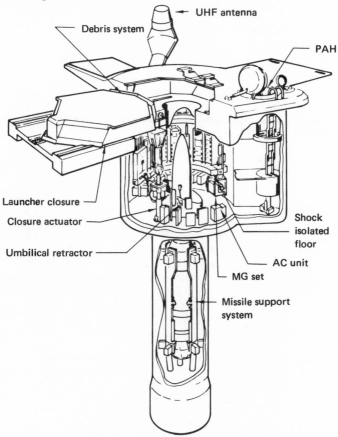

Fig. 1 − Launch facility

Because of their remote rural locations, the sites were supplied by power lines that were not designed for handling the heavy power demands of simultaneous air carbon arc gouging and welding operations. Consequently, severe power fluctuations raised havoc with the control of heat settings. Severe power drains also were experienced when irrigation pumps were turned on or at milking or supper time; however, after 10 pm, when the ranchers went to bed, the welding machine settings usually had to be reduced.

The bulk of the weld repair activities occurred throughout the launch equipment room, on the upper launch tube, and near the top of the lower launch tube. Welding occurred in all positions; FCAW with 0.045-inch diameter E70T-1 cored filler wire and 75% Ar-25% CO_2 shielding gas was the primary welding process, while SMAW with E7018 electrodes in 3/32- or 1/8-inch diameters was the secondary process for all applications. E6013 electrodes were used for the root pass when moisture was present. Weld power supplies and gas bottles were mounted in trailers above ground. Initially, the welders had only wire feed controls available at their work stations; later on, machines with remote voltage controls were obtained.

The latest issue of the site drawings dictated AWS D1.1-75 as the controlling structural steel welding code; hence, the repair activities would be keyed to its requirements. However, neither this, nor the more recent revisions of AWS D1.1, Structural Welding Code — Steel, contain more than 1-1/4 pages on the subject of repair of existing structure, and the treatment is very general indeed! Furthermore, there were no guidelines available to the engineers on setting up a repair program, the design decisions to be made, or the contents of the weld process specification. Consequently, our initial engineering approach was based upon our best understanding of the problem.

Initial Engineering

In the early stages of the structural analysis, a duplicate set of engineering drawings was modified to include a unique number in the tail of each weld symbol, so as to provide positive identification of each weld throughout the analysis and repair programs. These became the "locator" drawings with a unique drawing number. These drawings were not subject to any of the revisions occurring on the master drawings. Once the weld joints to be repaired were identified, two documents were prepared. The first was an inspection document that identified the inspection criteria for each weld; the second was a process specification to control the welding to satisfy the requirements of AWS D1.1-75.

Concurrent with the document development effort, a team of project, welding, and quality assurance engineers made a survey at one of the sites, physically identified each of the welds, affixed its number on masking tape beside the weld, and completely photographed the site. The photographic record was to be a most valuable tool in the months to come, permitting concerned parties in California, Washington, and Montana to converse in an intelligent manner about a given weld problem.

The primary objective of the site survey was to determine:

(1) How the weld would be inspected

(2) Accessibility to the joint for welding and inspection

(3) What equipment would be removed or required protection during the repair activities

(4) If the weld were to be removed, by what method (i.e., grinding or air carbon arc gouging)

(5) The welding method to be used, SMAW or FCAW

(6) The repair approach:
    (a) Increase the size of existing fillets
    (b) Remove and replace the weld
    (c) Add a second fillet weld on the opposite side of the part
    (d) Add additional fillet welds between existing welds
    (e) Add fillet welds on top of existing groove welds
    (f) Add shear bars
    (g) Remove and reinstall new hardware

There were to be several additional methods added, once repair activities got under way, including:

(h) Remove and repair sections of the structure containing one or more welds

(i) Install a secondary structure over the existing structure to carry all or part of the load

Following the site survey, changes were made in the two documents to allow for the conditions that had been observed, and the final release was made. Engineering planning was readied, the contractor got the welding crews together, and the program got under way.

Tango 49 — Face to Face with Reality

Site T-49 (Tango 49) was selected as the first site where we would verify our approach, make corrections to our documents, and then transfer our procedures to the next sites. Our plan was to eventually have simultaneous operations at 10 sites, two shifts per day. In August 1978, crews entered site T-49, pulled the missile and critical gear, shut down the electrical and cooling systems, and readied the site for the inspection team.

Where is Weld 125? A minor problem—but a very real one—started the program off. Where were all these welds located? The picture record, taken on the initial survey, was to prove its worth. The effort of identifying welds that had taken a crew of engineers a day-and-a-half to accomplish was achieved by one person in less than a day. All welds were identified with masking tape, a procedure that was repeated at the rest of the nine beginning sites to help the crews identify their job as it started. Once the welds were identified, the inspection program moved along at a fairly smooth pace; however, it quickly became apparent that this site had many conditions not observed in the site examined during our survey. It also became apparent as welding activities progressed that our process specification was inadequate and lacked the degree of flexibility needed. Many engineering change orders were written to cope with the many new problems encountered. Additional engineering documents also would be required that gave much more explicit instructions than our original planning had given. It should be pointed out, however, that our weld specifications and all our engineering and planning documents were based upon the concepts used in our shops and in our retrofit programs, which were appropriate for the task then at hand.

However, we were now dealing with corrective action in which the actual conditions were highly variable. Residual stresses in the parts produced totally unpredictable changes in the straightness of a joint edge once a defective weld had been cut out, and fillet welds were oversized or occurred on opposite sides from where they were to have been, according to the drawing. Excessive root gaps were commonplace, or the root opening along a given seam might vary as much as a half-inch because of the high residual stresses in the part. Our weld numbering system proved both a blessing and a disaster, for while it made location of a weld and planning for its rework easy, the fact that a number of welds were associated with any given part had not been fully considered when the engineering was prepared. It was apparent that the repair of all welds associated with a given part must be considered as a single repair problem.

Several other factors became readily apparent at this time, including the following:

(1) It would be faster and more cost effective to remove large sections of the structure containing several defective welds and establish new joint locations in virgin metal.

(2) It would be faster and more cost effective to totally remove and replace each weld and, in some cases, to install new structural elements than to try to rework and salvage the existing structure.

(3) For certain weld joints, the addition of shear bars or scab plates to provide alternate load paths would prove structurally efficient and cost effective.

(4) It is standard practice in the aerospace industry for the quality control department to prepare an unplanned event record when the item being built is not per drawing, cannot be processed according to specification, or is deficient in other respects. This is a costly and time-consuming procedure, and a method was required to reduce the number of unplanned event records that were being written. The process specification controls required greater flexibility.

(5)   Detailed construction procedures would be required to guide the iron workers installing the hardware. This was especially critical where preservation of part location was necessary when the structural element was under load.

(6)   The welders needed a better understanding of the task and close engineering support when problems arose.

Re-engineering the Job. The revised engineering proved highly effective, and a very high-quality repair was accomplished at each site. As the crews gained experience, quality, cost of repair, and time schedules improved at each new site. The changes that took place included the following:

(1)   The weld process specification was rewritten to provide the required flexibility to cope with the actual conditions, yet still maintain control of the process and ensure conformance with AWS D1.1 and drawing requirements.

(2)   Detailed repair procedures covering each weld or combination of welds were prepared.

(3)   A welder training program was set up to provide welders with better familiarization with the task at hand.

(4)   As our familiarity with the site conditions improved, two separate crews were established to prepare the sites ahead of the welders. These included:
  (a)   A line-burning crew that did the major portion of the cutting operations for installation of the new plates
  (b)   An air carbon arc cutting crew that removed the bulk of the defective welds

Weld Process Specification – Flexibility and Control. The initial repair weld specification paralleled the specifications used in our shops and in the field construction environment involving new hardware. Because these are relatively rigid welding environments, the specifications did not require a great deal of flexibility. However, the high degree of variation occurring in the repair situation required the specification to have an inherent flexibility. The most critical problems include:

(1)   Weld procedures where there is a wide range of root gaps along a single weld joint in both fillet and groove welds

(2)   Weld procedures for full penetration groove welds where the weld may be accessible for only part of its length

(3)   Weld joints where accessibility has been totally impaired on one side by equipment that cannot be removed

(4)   Changes in joint configurations caused by actual site contours

(5)   Seal welding

Once these problems were addressed and the inspectors had well-defined controls that could be applied to most situations, the welding pace quickly increased.

The most common problem involved root gaps varying from 0 to 1/2 inch along the same joint. While the drawing might show a full penetration groove weld with a backing beam (maximum root gap 3/16 inch), the specification permitted a temporary backing bar to be installed along that portion of the weld where the gap exceeded 3/16 inch. Additional rules were applied to joints where accessibility was restricted on the back side to either permit backing bars to be left in place or for a full penetration groove weld to be made from one side only. The specification also was to allow for the optional use of ceramic backing material on groove welds.

Due to settling that had occurred over the years, the once level floors and ceilings now had significant unevenness in them. When the burning crews would set up to make parallel cuts in the liner plates for the installation of new liner plates, they might be 1 inch off the floor at one point and on the floor at another. The specification provided rules for installing the required full penetration groove along such a seam.

Other rules were included in the specification covering numerous other, but less critical, variations, such as the use of E6013 electrodes for seal welding when moisture was present.

Detailed Repair Instructions – The Key to Success. Although a high degree of controlled flexibility was achieved in the weld process specification, more information was required for the installation of each weld or welded assembly. Because additional information was required relative to the repair of each individual weld, we elected to prepare a set of subtier documents with detailed instructions, subordinate to the weld process specification. Examples of the types of information provided by these documents are given in Figs. 2 and 3.

In Fig. 2, three options are provided for the repair of weld 256 (associated welds 257 and 258, which also exist on the same part, were repaired according to the same instructions). Regardless of the actual site conditions, the welders were now able to select an appropriate repair method.

In Fig. 3, the repair instructions for a new liner plate are given. Here, detailed welding sequences are provided so that distortion of the structure is minimized.

With the completion and release of each of the repair documents (five in all), the tempo picked up! The welding crews could now deal with the bulk of the conditions encountered with considerably less engineering support. (It was not uncommon for the welding engineer to log up to 350 miles per day to support welding crews at 10 sites.) As experience was gained, improvements were made to the instructions to simplify installation or to cover new or recurring conditions. In many cases, the welders provided significant input that made the job go faster, and the QC-1 inspections also added their input.

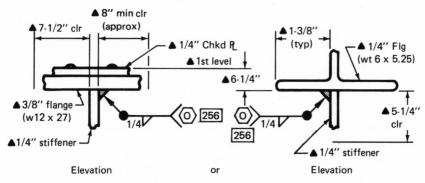

Elevation   or   Elevation

2nd level - beam stiffener (8 places)
(ESA room - underside of 1st level floor
AZ 115° & 140°)

▲REF ONLY

REMOVAL	
TORCH	☐
GRIND	☒
AAG	☒

INSTALLATION	
SMAW	☒
3/32	☒
1/8	☒
3/32	☐
(ROOT ONLY)	
FCAW	☒
.045	☒
.0625	☐
E7018	☐
(ROOT ONLY)	

▲ LENGTHS	
F—	0-24"
V—	H—
TOTAL	24"

Repair instructions

Note: Weld 256 shall be worked in conjunction with
Welds 257 & 258. Weld may exist on opposite side.

Method A) Repair-Opposite Side Accessible
1. Prepare surfaces on opposite side.
2. Install weld on opposite side per PDS Sheet 54.

Method B) Repair-Opposite Side Inaccessible
1. Remove stiffener & prepare surface angles.
or 2. Obtain stiffener P/N 24-9669-23 (6X8¼X¼)ASTM
A36. Install same location & trim to fit.
3. Install welds per PDS Sheet 54.

Method C) Repair-Opposite Side Inaccessible
1. Remove weld & prepare surfaces.
2. Install welds per PDS Sheet 54.

WELD REPAIR		SIZE	CODE IDENT NO.		21-60829
		A	81205		WELD # 256
CONST. DWG. 24-9772 SHT. 25		SCALE		REV G	SHEET 46
LOCATOR DWG. 24-9779 SHT. 32					

Fig. 2 – Optional repair procedures for fillet welded structure

8.6.5.4 -7 CUTOUT AND PLATE INSTALLATION

Repair instructions

Note: Before scribing outline, verify that welds 300, 301, 304, and 309 will be removed.

1. Remove stiffeners if applicable.
2. Make the -7 cutout.
3. Install new -7 plate and align for proper fit-up.
   a. Prepare all three/four edges of liner and plate for welding.
   b. Secure plate by dogging and/or tack welding on all sides.
4. Complete root pass on all three/four sides as applicable.
   a. Use backstepping technique for all sides.
   b. Weld in following sequence. (Viewed from launch tube side.)

   Note: Step 2) and 4) may be reversed.

   1) Left-hand vertical seam $\boxed{857}$.

   Use runoff tab at bottom of seam.

   Stop short or wraparound corner approximately 2 inches at top of seam.

   Note: Steps 2) and 3) may be reversed.

   2) Lower horizontal seam $\boxed{856}$.

   Weld progression shall be towards -6 plate area if -6 plate is not installed.

   Backpass from ler side first is recommended, then backgouge from launch tube side.

   Stop short approximately 2 inches from right-hand corner.

   Use runoff tab on left-hand corner.

   3) Upper horizontal seam $\boxed{855}$.

   Weld progression shall be towards -6 plate area, if -6 plate is not installed.

   Stop short approximately 2 inches from -12 cutout, if -12 plate will be installed next.

   Install runoff tab at umbilical opening. Weld cut seam to umbilical opening if -12 plate is in place.

   4) Weld right-hand vertical $\boxed{854}$ if -6 is in place.

5. While keeping dogs and/or tacks in place, weld out all front seams complete.
   a. After welding of root pass on all three/four seams, each seam may be completed individually or at the same time.
   b. Stagger starts and stops in multipass welds.
   c. Backstepping mandatory, but backstepping length optional.
   d. Stop short or wraparound corners approximately 2 inches, as defined in step 4.

6. Backgouge by AAG and/or grinding to sound metal if necessary. Weld backside if necessary. Weld out all back seams complete per 5a, 5b, 5c, 5d above. Backgouging may be accomplished simultaneously with backgouging of -5 and -6 plates.

Fig. 3A — Repair instruction for distortion control during linear plate installation

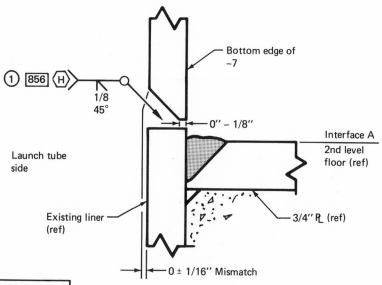

Bottom edge of
–7

① 856 Ⓗ

1/8
45°

0″ – 1/8″

Interface A
2nd level
floor (ref)

Launch tube
side

Existing liner
(ref)

3/4″ ℞ (ref)

0 ± 1/16″ Mismatch

REMOVAL	
TORCH	☒
GRIND	☒
AAG	☐

INSTALLATION	
SMAW	☒
3/32	☒
1/8	☒
3/32	☐
(ROOT ONLY)	
FCAW	☒
.045	☒
.0625	☐
E7018	☐
(ROOT ONLY)	

LENGTHS (REF)	
F–	0–
V–	H 96″
TOTAL	96″

① Back pass from ler side first
is recommended, then back gouge
from launch tube side
Optional: Weld per JWP FEFCA00036
when root gaps between 1/4″ & 5/16″ exist.

REPAIR INSTRUCTIONS:

1. WORK IN CONJUNCTION WITH WELDS 854, 855, &
   857.

2. SEE PARA. 8.6.5.4 FOR REPAIR INSTRUCTIONS.

WELD REPAIR		SIZE	CODE IDENT. NO.	21-60867
		A	81205	WELD # 856
CONST. DWG.	SHT.			
LOCATOR DWG.	SHT.	SCALE	REV C	SHEET 164

Fig. 3B — **Repair instructions for weld joints with
variable root gaps**

Welder Training — A Must

While many of the welders hired for the repair program had previous experience with the FCAW process, some were using semiautomatic welding machines for the first time. Air carbon arc gouging was new to many, and since the requirements for removal of defective welds were fairly stringent, a training and qualification program was established.

A private consultant set up a day-long class for each of the welding crews, completely reviewing the basics of the FCAW process and some of the more basic problems encountered. In addition, impromptu training sessions took place at the sites when a particularly sticky problem was encountered by a crew. The benefits of the training program, plus the close support of the welders by the welding engineers, showed rapid payoff. Morale picked up, and productivity and quality increased. Quality assurance implemented a welder report card system that proved highly beneficial. It permitted us to isolate welders having technique problems and allowed us to work with them to correct their deficiencies. It also gave the welder a record of his accomplishments.

Separation of Activities — Improved Productivity

At the beginning of the program, an overly cautious approach was taken with regard to the extent of defective weld that could be removed from each joint; thus, each welder prepared his weld joints as he went. With the changes introduced into the weld process specification and with increased experience, we were able to set up three site preparation crews that moved into the sites in front of the welding crews to accomplish a large portion of the preparation work.

The first crew was the line burning crew, whose responsibility consisted of cutting the liner plates along the required locations. This consisted of making the cuts along a given line, leaving tabs 2 to 3 inches wide about every 2 feet. The cutouts thus remained in position and helped retain the structure in its existing position until installation of the new part was to occur. The second and third crews accomplished as much of the air carbon arc gouging of the defective welds as was deemed advisable, thus minimizing the amount of arc gouging to be accomplished by the welders. This was to have a significant effect on the morale of the welding crews for several reasons, one of the most important being related to the line power fluctuations, which were a never-ending problem. It also improved working conditions, cutting down on both noise and dust.

The Bottom Line — A Quality Product

When the last of the 50 sites was completed in November 1979, it was evident to all that the success of this program was brought about by five key factors:

(1) A weld process specification that had inherent controlled flexibility.

(2) Detailed engineering instructions were made available covering the repair of each joint with alternate repair methods that could be used to accommodate variations in the existing conditions.

(3) The welders were trained and were thoroughly knowledgeable in the process and equipment. Close engineering support was available at all times.

(4) Separation of line burning operations and a reduction in the amount of air carbon arc gouging accomplished by the welders significantly improved productivity.

(5) Involving the welders and weld inspectors in the "best way to repair" decisions where possible.

A sixth factor, perhaps one of the most important in the success of this program, was that it became a strong team effort with every group, from the welders to the Air Force engineering units, working in close harmony.

Guidelines for a Weld Repair Program

The lessons learned at the beginning of this program clearly indicate that successful and cost effective weld repair programs can be conducted. However, early success is based upon specification flexibility and the provision for optional approaches to be taken. It further emphasizes the need for detailed instructions for control of the operations. Leaving the welder to his own devices is a risky measure in any welding operation, but in repair operations it can prove to be disastrous. The principal elements that will ensure the success of a weld repair program involving existing structures are as follows:

(1) Provide positive identification of the welds to be repaired; develop a numbering or locating system that will provide easy reference on the drawings, in the planning, and on the part.

(2) Make a site survey; identify the parts to be repaired or replaced. Affix the identification to the part. Make a complete photographic record during the survey. Note accessibility to both sides of the part, and identify potential problem areas. Establish preliminary repair and inspection methods. Locate, if possible, welds that will not be repaired, assess their condition, and determine if their presence may be problematic.

(3) Draft a weld-repair-oriented process specification. Make provisions for optional repair methods to be used. Provide for variable root openings in both groove and fillet welds, provide measures for tying into old welds, and establish machine grounding requirements.

(4) Prepare preliminary repair plans for each weld or assembly. Consider optional approaches.

(5) Lay out the entire job by segments; establish sequencing of operations. Determine if repair methods established in item 4 are most feasible and consider alternate repairs such as prefabricating a subassembly containing several welds. Establish the feasibility of setting up specialty crews (e.g., line burners, air carbon arc crews) to speed up the job.

(6) Train your welders and inspectors.

(7) Make provisions for rapid revision of plans and specifications.

(8) Establish a nondestructive evaluation program with a statistical sampling plan.

A Final Point

The author's experience in setting up the engineering documents and in the actual conduct of the program clearly indicates the need for better, more definitive guidelines and code requirements than those currently given in AWS D1.1. The welding industry should consider establishing a strong set of rules and regulations for conducting repair programs, and provide engineers with guidelines as to the problems to be addressed in setting up repair programs.